Julia Crafts Smith

The Reason Why

Or, spiritual experiences of Mrs. Julia Crafts Smith, physician, assisted by her spirit guides

Julia Crafts Smith

The Reason Why
Or, spiritual experiences of Mrs. Julia Crafts Smith, physician, assisted by her spirit guides

ISBN/EAN: 9783337373443

Printed in Europe, USA, Canada, Australia, Japan

Cover: Foto ©Thomas Meinert / pixelio.de

More available books at **www.hansebooks.com**

THE REASON WHY;

OR,

SPIRITUAL EXPERIENCES

OF

MRS. JULIA CRA

PHYSIC

BY HE

B

PUBLISHED B

188

PREFACE.

All books, like individuals, have their place in this world, and serve a purpose, for the benefit of the race; and if this little volume, written by me, at the suggestion of a spirit father, cheers one despondent heart, I shall be amply paid. Of the criticisms it may meet, I have no fears, as I have not aspired to make this book great, but truthful. Neither do I boast of its merits as a scholarly production; it is only to encourage those who have been by circumstances denied an education; — and their aspirations have met with a ready response from the spirit world, through Inspiration.

I dedicate this book to J. A. and O. W. N——, for their kindness to me and mine in the past; — "I was sick and they visited me; an hungered, and they fed me ; in trouble they came unto me." And after I have passed from earth, may my life encourage them in all good works, and teach them, that out of God's abundance, comes all there is in the earth; that spiritual blessings are not made up of material things, but come as an influx out of the Spirit world.

JULIA C. SMITH.

INTRODUCTION.

Strange as it may seem to those unacquainted with the science of Spirit Communion, (although possibly believers in the immortality of the soul,) that after many years wandering in spirit life and spirit land, I return, and through my beloved child, write an introduction to a little work dedicated to my wife, M. A. Norcross, who in my young days fought the battle of life with me.

Though we differed much in our theological views, in consequence, it made us somewhat estranged in our spiritual belief; yet to me my earthly life bears a happy record, for the firmness of her with whom I was united, kept me, who was not only influenced by those in the body, but by those out of it,— acting as acted upon, ignorant of the why and wherefore, till I passed to the Spirit World. Then, as I met the Spirit Band, who had been watching and waiting, my mind unfolds to the truth, —*I was a Medium!*

And now, after years of anxious waiting, beholding my child buffeting the storms of life, under many difficulties, and by that discipline drawing nearer the spirit world, by desiring the rest and peace that comes therefrom,— opening her inner life to a spirit band, who have always, since her childhood, been watching the progress of her mental capacities, and holding such communications with her from time to time, as to fit and prepare her for a work for the benefit of humanity, and as I have had this work under contemplation for some time, and meeting with those who have a desire to assist in any *good work*, I hereby, with feelings of thankfulness to God, assist my daughter in putting forth a few SPIRITUAL TRUTHS.

JESSE S. NORCROSS.

THE REASON WHY.

CHAPTER I.

It is not all of life to live, simply; but all that is given to every child of earth, must be sown, like seed, to spring up among the children of men.

Thus and always, there will be those who are Phrenologically organized, to transmit, through the law of inspiration, truths to benefit the human race. But as long as Destiny rules the children of earth, and a Planetary Law in many ways govern them, just so long will it be necessary for Spirits to assist them to understand why they are here, and for what purpose; and while so many truths are hidden in the hearts of those God has seen fit to elect from the many, and they continue to hide their "lights under a bushel," just so long will Spirits come and throw their *positive* influence upon Mediums, to bring that truth to light, by acting upon every one who keeps from the world, that which a loving God sends through them, to those who are denied by nature inspirational knowledge; and it is time that they should have encouragement, by reading the experience of others from our realm, that it may be a guide to them, after Mediums like this, with many others, have passed to us. to receive the "Well done, thou good and faithful servant." Oh! the precious experiences of earth-life. Gems, hidden from the gaze of the many, locked up in the human soul, that should be brought out of the dark cells of your lives, to open the eyes and ears of those that live on the earth, to strengthen them, and teach them that the great vein of sympathy that runs through human life, cannot be broken by any *law*, that can possibly be made by man. Children of earth, why struggle against the God-given light that comes to you in your lonely hours, when unseen loved ones are hovering near, trying to give you light in the darkness which surrounds your spiritual vision. Remember, that as you spiritualize yourself by doing good to others, so you attract the loved ones, who are not *dead but gone before.*

Lingering upon, or near the earth in anxiety concerning my wife and children, and especially this child, whose mediumistic powers attracted me to her, and gave me the power of progressing more rapidly in my spirit home, by bringing those missionaries in spirit life to me, whose great desire was to do good to those in the earth life, — and feeling that my influence over my darling child would open the gateway through her mental faculties much easier than any influence that was strange to her, as she might repulse them at any time: — for be assured that the will of a mental medium can always prevent her being controlled or entranced.

It seems but yesterday that I left Boston, and wife and children, to wander after gain in a strange land. My last night in Boston was passed in this child's home, and the vision of her trials and cares came up before me. But in the same vision I beheld her triumphantly putting all her troubles behind her, and moving on with a band of bright spirits bearing three flags, — Spiritual Strength, Mental Activity, and Intellectual Growth. Many other scenes came up before me. My sister, also, (who had appeared to me years before), assuring me of her care and love, but telling me that I would never return to my home again; as my home in the spirit world was most ready for me. Oh! the mental agony of that day in the A.D. 1850. I did not dare to tell my wife, as she did not believe in any of the so-called superstitions which I entertained; her physical health being poor, I tried to believe it was a dream occasioned by my sad feelings at leaving home and family.

I had in years gone by seen my sister many times, and she had proven to me beyond a doubt, of the *existence* of our loved ones, in a future life. But owing to my wife's bigotry and orthodox views, I was obliged to keep in my inner life, many things which might have hastened the coming light that earth's children now enjoy. It was my sister Belle coming to me, and what she said, that made me take up the bodies of my brothers and sisters, sometime buried, and burn them to stay the ravages of consumption in my family, which was a success, no one having died of that disease for forty-five years. I think now that her first visit to me, and her free conversation with me occurred in A.D. 1829, also in 1831; and again in 1833. But receiving opposition from those who did not have the power to see what I saw, and desiring peace instead of war, I sometimes rushed into anything to keep me from seeing or thinking of the many wonderful things which were open to my spiritual vision. But when the Bible was brought into consideration by those of a different belief, it was then that my very soul was stirred within me, and I felt that if there was more love and truth, there would be less discord in earth life; and I have not changed my mind in that respect, though a sojourner in spirit life thirty years. Many years before I had promised my wife that if I died first, I would come and tell her if my belief in Universal Salvation was true or false. And if she passed away first she also was to come (if permitted to return, which she did not believe), and tell me if there was a Hell for unfortunate spirits. But it was my destiny to open the gateway of spirit communion between her spirit and mine, by passing away first.

Away from home and friends in a strange land, where civilization had not her laws enforced, men were more like vampires or demons, than men; heeding not the Christian precepts of "loving your neighbor as yourself," or of "ministering unto him when he is sick," as God has commanded in His record.

When will Spirituality so far overcome the evil in men's natures, that they will not be forgetful of the spirit within the casket of clay, and contribute to its needs rather than looking only to see how much they may be enriched, by what little wordly goods they may die possessed of.

Believe me, I have no desire to dwell upon my sufferings or mental agony in my dying moments; suffice it to say, that all the gold in the mines of California, if within my control, I would have freely given, to have felt the hand of my beloved wife or children, and to hear words of love and kindness, from those who were dearer to me than life. And let me say, dear reader, to all: cherish the love of relations and friends on earth, remembering it is only love and spirituality that can be taken from this material abode. And the spirit is poor indeed, when entering spirit life, if poverty of spirit exist within them; and still worse if they have so lived, that no loving soul sends up from earth, that longing and loving telegram to bring us to them. Oh! man and woman, seek to cover the faults of your friends, and search diligently for all the good, that it may bring out of them all the good, and help to overcome all that is evil in their natures; that by-and-by when they or you have passed on, the connecting link of love may be the railroad on which the spirit can return, and that it was well that you had lived, and also well, that you passed over, according to a law in nature.

But God in His goodness never gave any one a cup of sorrow unmixed with joy. Oh! no; and my agony at being separated from my loved ones, was, as soon as I had passed from my body, and become emancipated from pain and suffering, well repaid by meeting my darling children, brothers and sisters; and that sister who had many times stood at my side while I was in the form, was there to give me welcome, and assure me that I could fulfill my promise to those I had left in the flesh.

Oh! heavenly thought; out of the darkness of despair and suffering, into the light of love and happiness. Spiritual light. But those greetings and thoughts were of short duration, as love being the stronger element in my nature, I began to ask myself, what my family would say, when not receiving a letter or word from me; and I only thought it, when Belle, who read my inner life best, said to me, "Jesse, you remember how I came to you? Go to them in the same way, and relieve their anxiety concerning your silence. I can assist you." And amidst all the beauties of my spirit entrance, I had not changed my mind, but still had a desire to return and fulfill my promise. I did not find it hard to do, as my longing was so great, and with my sister I journeyed homeward. It seemed a long time; but to my astonishment I was told I had only been out of the body thirteen hours, before I was striving to make them understand that I was there, bereft of all that belonged to my physical life, endeavoring, by every faculty I could put forth, to arrest their attention. I had also the carefulness to not wish to frighten those I wanted to reach. I have since learned from Willie, who has come to me, (but was then in the physical body,) that he beheld me by his medium powers, and that my wife was truly convinced I was there, by my attempts to use a drum, which was mine, and that I used to use, before leaving home for California,— which she acknowledged by changing her views for a more rational theological belief. I was then informed by my brother James, that my daughter Julia was destined to become an avenue for spiritual manifestation, through her mental faculties, and that I was called home to assist in the work, as being nearer and dearer to her. I might, through my death, bring her nearer to light and life; and I, with others, stood beside her, letting into her life the words of inspiration, and a new growth, for twelve years, before we could herald forth that a new worker was in the vineyard, declaring God's goodness to his children. But still I assure you, we are cognizant of the fact, that all development comes through suffering, and many years of this medium's life, physically, were used up to sustain her brain. But out of the discipline of her suffering, we knew would come a benefit, not only to herself, spiritually, — but by her election for her work; we, her guides, well knew we could assist suffering humanity. For, my dear reader, let me here say to you, that whomsoever is elected by the Celestial Spheres, to serve as servants to the spirit world, are elected from their infancy, and will accomplish the work assigned to them. They may suffer in mind and body, but the work they are fitted for is an especial work, and must be done; we must have avenues laid out, through which to communicate, (or to travel;) sacrifices must be made; and if through the peril of life, the chosen one gets disheartened, there must another tie be broken, another chair be vacant, or another cradle be empty, to bring the medium's spirit heavenward. So you can see link after link was broken, that my darling child might look up, and health fail her, that she might loose her hold on earthly things, and come up higher in thought and feeling; and when life became irksome to her, and sadness and sorrow seem to surround her, and the physical was weakened with disease, and deception and the false-heartedness of those whom she had loved best, came up before her, then, and not till then, did we get her to yield to our influence, and to do the work as it must be done. I think that was about A.D. 1863, that we felt we had accomplished a work *we could praise God for;* she being then about thirty-one years old. Now, let me say here, that all true mediums, are chosen, because they have organizations adapted to the use of those workers who desire to accomplish a good work on your plain.

And I would here say to those readers of this, that no one, either high or low, learned or unlearned, should in anywise condemn, or abuse one of these chosen ones, no matter whatsoever your opinion of the case may be, unless you can first understand the working of God's mighty law in spirit life. You have not any right to judge, lest you bring upon yourself a mighty judgment for your unbelief.

How can you believe in a God you have not seen, if you do not render justice to his chosen ones, who take up the crosses of life, and bear them patiently, meeting with scoff and scorn, knowing that they are sustained by the light you know nothing of. At this time, my daughter's health was so frail, that we desired her to recover, to begin the great work before her. And I, being chosen to manifest myself in such manner as to encourage her, and also to give her physical health and strength, and such information cerning what was desired of her, and to get from her a promise to dedicate her life to our work, which she did, and has done, regardless of opposition, or lack of encouragement or material aid. But as one of God's laws is, "as you sow so shall ye also reap," so in due time she shall reap more abundantly than she has sown; and the many of God's children she has in no wise turned away, so shall it be meted out to her and hers, as she has measured to others.

About the time we began to control her, and use her brain, and encourage her to stand at the post of duty, she was communicating with me. One evening I told her her brother William should not go to California, that he would never return if he did; but he, like all who hear the word and do not believe, went to California; any other country would have been better. As his planetary law gave him Jupiter as a metal in his composition, the coming to a country where metal was then a condition in the elements, he, also, in accordance with the laws of accident, came to spirit life. Finding a work begun, he, with all his strength of youth and manhood, swung wide open the door between the physical and spiritual world. He, having a surplus of vitality to use, having passed out of the body in full strength, and mother, sisters and friends, became interested in the work we had begun; and it has ever been his end and aim to assist in the duties assigned her.

How little is known of the connection, or links, that bind the spirit world to this! How many false theories are advanced by the theological world, and the workers who advance their ideas. If they were only obliged to bring proof of what they put forth, there would not be so much that is not reasonable, or so many false ideas advanced; but every one would be obliged to give a reason for the faith that is in them; and it would give mediums an opportunity to give more explanation concerning the mediumistic life, which they do not choose themselves, but who are chosen by unseen ones. And instead of being treated as if it was something to their discredit, their friends should rejoice that they have even one who is God's chosen disciple; — for most any medium can prove that spirits do return to the earth. But I deny the power of any theologian, to prove by his theology, that spirits ever leave the earth.

Ah! reader, remember that God's laws are unchangeable; and you or yours may be called for some especial work, in due time, and there is no power on earth to prevent, when it is once decided on our plain.

Those dear guardian angels, who have walked side by side from their earliest infancy, know best who is fitted for the work. And it is their report to the angelic hosts that makes the chosen ones of God. Acts, x.: 34, 35. And what God has chosen, say thou is not fit to fill the place that he has assigned them, and *must be filled.* Read what the voice said to Peter and be silent. Acts, xi.: 5—9.

After my son William came to us, his desire was to be in rapport with his sister; and for three years, long and faithful, did he traverse earth-plain by her side, interesting her in all good works which he was interested in while on earth.

But those guides that formed her medical band, held her to her promise, to relieve the sick and suffering everywhere; and also to bear testimony to the truth of spirit communion, and God's universal love, to the children of men, and taught her to fear not the inquisition of public opinion; for any one who interests themselves in any good work, must expect the lash of censure, as long as there is so much ignorance and sensualism on your earth. Men, until they are pure themselves, can never see purity in others; they believe what they see and hear, and realize, by their perverted senses; never suspecting that the diseases of the physical body, so affect the mental and moral nature, that correct judgment, or unbiased, is an impossibility.

When we see the greatest blessings perverted by those who should be instructors for good, instead of feeding the lower faculties of man, it makes me ask, what of the coming future? And who has the moral courage, to weed out from the press and pulpit, those evils that are undermining and corrupting society? Is it to be wondered at, that falsehood and deception, scandal and sensualism, hypocrisy and deceit are running riot in your midst, when your daily and weekly papers are filled with rottenness and slime, fed out without stint to the masses at two and three cents a day? Great heavens! will men never understand the great principle of life: that a lie is a lie! told for nothing or money, it makes no difference. A thief is a thief! no matter whether he steals millions of money, or the reputation of his fellow man or woman. It is not what he takes from his earthly possessions; *that* all comes out of God's bounteous stores; but the eternal principle of truth is perverted.

There would be no need of so much unnecessary material used to build lofty edifices, to stand out as a sign of a wicked and immoral race. It is not expensive churches that come up to spirit life, but the true and sincere souls that worship within their walls. Beautiful edifices, transplanted on your plain, sent forth to the mighty and noble intellects of earth, through receptive inspiration from our world!

But why not make the worshippers true and earnest men and women, by giving them the truthful assurance, that there are unseen intelligences recording the spirituality of their lives? What man or woman was ever any worse, for believing in a good or loving God, and the ministrations of their unseen friends? If we are honest with ourselves, and have no sins to hide, we have nothing to fear.

What man was ever any better for a belief in annihilation, or that ignored the cause that produces the effects that you see around you in earth-life? What mother feels happier to know that her babe has gone into some vegetable life, or to perdition for the lack of baptism?

When the mighty truth of spiritualism gives comfort to a lonely heart, and assures the mother of a meeting with her loved ones by-and-by, why cling to theories that degrade the true principle of life. All theories which represent God as an angry father, or revengeful, not only degrade the believer, but the God whom they worship; and all those who desire annihilation, or try to build up a belief that there is no life beyond this earth of yours, must lose sight of that astronomical phenomenon, which the starry world proclaims nightly to earth's children's short vision.

Better believe in your transit to other and larger planets, that are swinging in space, than to doubt the goodness of God, or his ability to care for his children, without sending them to perdition; with no chance of progressing. Man did not come here of his own accord, and in consequence, is not responsible for the place he shall occupy hereafter.

Why do men study so hard to believe anything but the simple truth, because they are striving to "climb up some other way," than by learning one great truth, simple as it is, that there is no death, all is life, nothing is lost, but all is changing and going on through all eternity under a law of evolution.

But I stray from my purpose in writing this. It is to show why my child or any other is obliged to walk in a way peculiar to a mediumistic life, amidst thorns and thistles, bearing many crosses, meeting opposition that must arise in such a life; but by-and-by they will learn, that where roses grow, thorns must abide, and both will be found growing side by side.

But, fond mother, though there is no consolation given you by others, we come to tell you that your darling child will be well cared for, nourished and fed by loving ones in the summer land. And if your love is the true mother's love, and you miss its loving smile and tiny form — by that law you hold him or her, in your atmospheric surroundings, until such time as it can leave you, without giving you loneliness of spirit. Still, if you feel that those little ones are a burden to you, they will not stay with you, but will wing their way where they are not an unwelcome guest.

Would you behold the real mourners in the spirit life? They are those whose friends have draped themselves in black to show to an indifferent world what a loss they have met with, and forgetful of the link of affection, which is the only chain that can unite them on earth or in spirit life. To die and be forgotten by your friends is enough to make sad any sensitive soul. Think of your loved and lost ones, and the telegraph you send out from your spirit, will not only benefit you, but those who have passed on, to realize the quickening of the love element, in their spirit home.

> **Oh! to mourn and miss a loved one!**
> **'Tis a right that God has given;**
> **And it is a chain that links us**
> **To a home, that's ours, in Heaven.**

CHAPTER II.

It may seem strange, at a time like the present, when the human race are laboring under so many changes, and strife and discord seem to rule the hour, and perfect confidence seems to be a principle of the past, that we should desire to bring our mite into existence, to assist and encourage those who are disheartened, and who are in the depths of doubt, and fast verging into the channels of despair. There never was a time, when so many souls were sending up their spirits, asking the whys and wherefores of life.

In the past ages, dark ignorance made them submit to the higher authorities; but to-day every one thinks for themselves, and fast travel out from under the old superstitions and terrible creeds that bound them. The old tortures of the past are fast going out on both continents, for a new era to come in, to bless the children of God. And why not? Have there not been blood shed enough? Has there not been crimes enough committed? Has there not been suffering enough? Have not the innocent and the poor been crushed enough to satisfy this monster, "The Established Church," that would take away the liberties from the people, and compel them to think and act according to its dogmas?

Who gave them all knowledge? Not God, to be sure! for the diversity of opinion is necessary to mental growth; and not any of them have ever been to the spirit world, to gain knowledge which they can positively affirm is true.

How dare they presume that God has given them any more spiritual knowledge than he has the humblest of his creatures? *Jesus was chosen from the lowly.* And why? Because false knowledge gained, would have been an impediment to the inspiration of God's truth.

If it was not for your liberal government of to-day, your religions, based upon the atonement, would be no better than in the past. Keep God out of the constitution of state and nation, if you do not wish the inquisition of the past. He belongs, not in the constitution of nations, but in your souls.

It is those liberal minds who have revered God most, and loved the children of earth best, that have permeated your religious systems, until they are as tolerant as we find them to-day.

So, give yourselves no credit for your liberality; it was the law of force, — not that of love, as it should have been; and believe me, you will reap your reward.

In bringing this simple offering before her friends, I must take up many links of her life, and try to arrange a chain of circumstances and truths, that will encourage all the chosen mediums of God, that they may not fall by the wayside of life, but persevere unto the end; for out of the darkness of the past, comes a great light for the future.

No man or woman can rise above the masses, spiritually or mentally, but must expect to be a mark to be shot at continually, by those who do not, and those who will not understand them. For, until the bands of ignorance are broken, those laboring under its galling chains, will cry fraud, as their souls are in the prison of unbelief. Inspiration now, as in olden times, gives a mortal being precedence in your world; and that very precedence will create enemies among the ignorant and malicious. Men and women should learn the lesson well taught by one who suffered persecution from his fellow men. That knaves or fools were not troubled with enemies, so to meet obstacles and overcome them, shows spiritual growth, as it strengthens the mental and moral nature. Opposition is a natural growth, and walks side by side with Progression. All experience teaches us, that knowledge is the only key that can unlock for you the Kingdom of Heaven; and, as it is, nearly two thousand years have passed, and you are still groping in darkness concerning the spirit world; for ignorance still flaunts her banner, regardless of the fact, that struggling up out of the darkness is a mighty truth. The science of spirit communion, saying to the people of earth, try to understand the law of your physical bodies, for they are the temple of the spirit, and the mistakes of the past have been from a lack of information concerning the relation that exists between the mental, spiritual and physical bodies. Reason has been dethroned, to give way to selfishness and hypocrisy, until your nation seems to be a nation of hypocrites, who have lost faith in themselves and also in their fellow men.

Why this terrible dilemma of to-day? It is because mammon, and injustice, and a lack of spirituality in mortals, and want of possession where there is so much profession, is filling the world with woe. And if it was not for some of your silent and unobtrusive workers that are always sending up to the spirit world, their thanksgiving and praise, and throwing their magnetic influence into your life for good, you might realize a Sodom and Gomorrah as in olden times.

Why not understand this? That the law that unites the electric and magnetic forces on your earth, is a harmonic law, and well studied, will bring happiness to all who desire to promote the happiness of their fellows. Would it not be well to understand that the book of nature, united with the eternal book of intuition, solves more scientific problems, than all the congresses of scientists in the world?

Away back in the past, how boldly men advocated, suffered, and died, to promulgate a truth; and those truths lived. But behold the numberless errors that were sent forth by men who considered themselves and their doctrines infallible, which present experience teaches were not only *false*, but worthless; and earth's children, to-day, are suffering from their ignorance and wicked willfulness. For instance, the treatment of the sick; by administering poisons, burning and bleeding, cauterizing, blistering, cupping, salviating and torturing to make the sick well. And to-day another extreme comes before you; not so much suffering attending, but equally as dangerous, — bromides, morphine, hydrate of chloral, arsenicum, iron and minerals of any kind, — ignoring mother nature's ever soothing balm, the herbal creation, which was intended to affect and cure the diseases of mankind.

What right has any set of men, or scientists, to give poison to human beings, to destroy the physical body and dwarf the brain, and leave the poison in the system to be transmitted to unborn innocence, and call that curing the sick? There never was a dose of poison administered to the human body, but that was worse than the disease itself, your learned doctors to the contrary notwithstanding. It is a libel on the name of truth. No man living can tell you how mineral poisons are going to act on human bodies, as with different temperaments and constitutions, they act differently on different persons, under the law of absorption. Your lunatic asylums are being filled with human beings, made insane by transmitted poisons, and by treatment with bromides, hydrate of chloral, morphine, etc., and by poisonous applications, made to sensitive organs, which never should receive such harsh treatment; for the sympathy with, or between the lower organs and the brain and mammal glands, not only produce insanity but cancers. Don't you know that all diseases come on through the nervous system, and cannot be cured by sedatives? For the nervous system is the law of circulation, sensation and feeling.

If men had never doctored female diseases, you would not have so many insane women. And if men had behaved better, there would not be so much insanity amongst them from the prostration of the nerve centers.

There is so much indolence among a certain class of physicians, that they do not use their reason or experience, but prescribe for their sick and suffering patients, some worthless mineral or chemical preparation, not knowing whether it is adapted to their physical bodies or not. Believe me, they are responsible for the life they trifle with, and in spirit life will meet those whom they have assisted out of their bodies before their time. Verily they shall reap what they have sown.

Awake, intelligent men and women! Understand so well your own bodies, that you cannot be made the dupe of any class of physicians, though they have passed in, and also out of a medical college, and write M.D. after their names. They, too, may die with hydrophobia, from taking their own medicine. God makes His own doctors and ministers by intuition, and inspiration; the one will not fail you, nor rob you, nor the other *fall* to disgrace you; but drawing their strength from a higher source, will always feel the responsibility that rests upon them, thanking God, that He blesses their endeavors to do His work upon poor suffering humanity, their wounds constantly open, their sighs ever coming up from earth, and their wretched wail never ceasing. Annihilation is better for the man or woman, who at any time fill their coffers, by crushing one of those God's suffering and sin-sick souls. Beware, children of earth, gold will melt, silver will tarnish, but charity and love endureth forever

CHAPTER III.

TO THOSE WHO WOULD BE MEDIUMS.

It has been said that "a word to the wise is sufficient." And I would say to persons desiring to become mediums, you know not what you seek; if it comes to you, and you cannot escape it, bear patiently the cross that is put upon you; but if you use well your reasoning powers, you will never seek to become developed as a medium; for in your anxiety to become what you were never intended to be, you will find you are helping your own self to do what looks so easy when performed by natural mediums. Toil as you may, you can never be anything but a counterfeit; and in consequence will believe all others to be the same; to be sure all persons have some mediumistic powers, but all have not an organization adapted to use—and those powers better lie dormant, than to be developed when there is no balance power in the brain.

Look into the faces of some of the mediums who have forced their powers to the surface. They are only used to be fed upon by spirit vampires, who see and hear and know what is going on in the earth, by using the vitality from their physical bodies, regardless whether they live or die. They are spirits of low condition, who would not do better on earth, and will drag you down to their level. They can degrade you, but you can never lift them up; and when you think you have done so, you have brought some will-power stronger to bear upon them, and they have left, and given place to another. They have a better chance than you to advance, if they wish, and it is a wrong idea that you can lift them up out of their condition, consequent upon evil deeds while in the body. For when they come to your physical body, they bring with them their misdeeds; and you ofttimes become familiar with their sins, so they do not look so sinful to you; and you feel that you have elevated them — when in fact, you have sunk to their level. If you doubt this, ask any sincere man or woman who has investigated this subject, and have been in the habit of sitting with different kinds of mediums; they must either say, that some mediums are very low, or attach the blame to their influence. I have watched from my side, and find oftentimes that between the person whom the medium sits for, and the spirit who controls them, they are swamped, and go down to the perdition of circumstances. So I say, beware! there is danger in a mediumistic life, that is eagerly sought after. No honest *medium* will tell you that they would choose such a life for themselves, had they their choice. Ah, no! there is mental agony, fear of losing one's own individuality, and the being influenced at all times, and under trying circumstances, and tortured mentally by the spirit of strangers, wishing to warn their friends through the medium, — wishing you to go to them, and do many things that are quite impossible, and so depressing the medium, that at times it unfits them for any thing. And the more selfish the spirit was while in the body, the more they will make a useless machine of you.

See the medium whose health is destroyed, whose mind is diseased, whose control will abuse them, by twisting them in fearful contortions, and seem to delight in so doing. Do you believe these were sent by guardian angels? No! you are fearfully deceived. Are you not told to try the spirits, and see if they are not of God? If they are, they will not make a wreck of you, or say or do that which will disgrace you, or pervert your mental powers with low and vile influences which they bring, nor take the power of speech away from innocent children, cause epilepsy, or imitate engines, throw men down upon the sidewalk, and do all these wicked things, until they destroy the physical body of the *person*, only leaving them to attack some one else. These are demons, sent from your world by accident, murder, and by the law, and carry with them their revengeful feelings, and think no more of taking your body and using it up, than they would think of taking your pocket-book, or whatever belonged to you, if they were here; for, as a "tree falleth so it lies." I write this, because it is time you understood it; and this medium has the moral courage to send it out as a warning.

You will have to build mad-houses as plenty as school-houses, soon, if you do not learn that all medicines that make dormant the *will-power* of human beings, makes them negative; (as it is the *will* that protects them from spirits in the body or out of the body, and makes you maintain your own individuality.) Such medicines are opening the door to let in those unhappy beings on your plain, who will not spare any one which will meet their wants; and they can handle those best, who do not know, or believe in spiritualism, because it is called disease.

What your government should do, is to look into this science, and see if there are not some persons amongst you, who, having a strong will, a sympathetic soul, and faith enough in God and His ministering angels, to cast out these evil spirits. But as long as you send out from earth, human beings strangled by law, to get rid of them, which you do not, but only make them vindictive, you had better have a dozen in prison than one in spirit, going around, wreaking vengeance upon the innocent and negative.

Where are those who believe in the immortality of the spirit? *How dare* they uphold hanging for crime? Does not their belief in immortality show to them and to the world, that they, too, are committing a crime? Hanging sinners is not the best way to make saints; — taking away the life you cannot give, and sending spirits out of the body with all their material strength, (not having been wasted by disease), which they can use to wreak vengeance upon the dwellers of earth. Is it any wonder you have so much insanity, so many suicides and murders? Beware, lest the transgression of God's laws react to your sorrow.

I reiterate again, be careful about sitting in promiscuous circles. It is not only unhealthy, but dangerous, as you may attract some evil disposed person to you, who will throw their disease upon you, and enslave you by their influence, as many suffering ones on your earth can testify to-day. There are those on your earth, who are kept from the lowest dens of life by the law of force in your land, so we are obliged to leave them to a similar law in the spirit world; and you cannot blame your superior guides, for if you go into the mud, you must expect to get soiled. That is a law you cannot change.

There is a science about this that does not seem to be understood. For instance, two mediums can have slate writings, and other manifestations together, when if they separate, neither can have any; as the brain of one balances the powers in the other; and oftentimes, after separating, in trying to produce singly, what it took two to show, resort to fraud and trickery; and that is the reason why there is so much chaff to be sifted out, in order to get at the real truth, or genuine manifestations.

J. S. N.

CHAPTER IV.

To give an unpopular truth to the world, requires a large amount of moral courage; and also backbone enough to stand by whatever one may think and feel; — and not always to depend upon the five senses, but as many more as can be given through the individuality of some of the children of earth. There are those who think they know it all; but it has been my experience, as I have moved around in my humble way amongst the children of men, that there is no one so learned, that they cannot obtain some mighty and wholesome truths, from even the humblest of God's creatures; and my life with all its seeming mysteries in the past, has begun to be an open book to me, wherein I can read the fated stars that rule my life. Born of religious parents, who ever taught me that principle was a mighty power, and whose religious sentiments differed very much, they did not agree in opinions or creeds; they early taught their children the necessity of overcoming evil with good; and I bless the day and hour, when my father, with his love and belief in universal salvation, taught us, that if we placed our hands on the burning coals, no prayer or faith could allay the smart; and impressed upon our minds the necessity of living up to the "Golden Rule," which he always practiced, — "Love your neighbor as yourself;" that neighbor the whole world. Is it any wonder, that under such instruction, we should feel that Universalism was the true religion to bless mankind? Be that as it may; our mother was an Orthodox in her religious views, and we inherit from her, that positive principle, and strong element in our natures, that when we give a truth, we adhere to it with the tenacity of life. She also believed she was right, and all through her married life, that was the discordant element which hung as a cloud about our home; but as time wore on, my mother's health gave indication of an early death; and under those circumstances, father exacted a promise from my mother, that if she passed away first, she would return, if possible, and tell him which was the true religion, the Congregationalist belief, or universal salvation. In time mother recovered her health, and the question of theology was not referred to by either; as they had agreed to disagree on all religious subjects.

In the spring of the year 1850, my father left Boston in the ship Nestor, bound for California; and the next fall, in November, the night before Thanksgiving, mother was startled, after retiring to bed, by raps all about her room; and also brother Willie, who was a young lad, was awakened, and saw father standing beside his bed. He told mother, in a frightened way, that father was looking him in the face, and how dreadful sick he looked. The next day, Thanksgiving, was a sad day, indeed; for mother believed he was dead, and had returned to her, to assure her of his death, and also to fulfill the promise made years before that he would return if he passed away first.

He not only rapped in different places about the room, but a drum, on which he had often played to interest his children, was handled and played upon in a way and manner so like father, that we all became convinced that it was he.

This manifestation changed the whole current of my mother's life, and affected her so, spiritually, that she sent for the Universalist minister, Rev. E. F——, of Salem, Mass., he being settled there, and got his advice. He proved worthy of her confidence, for in less than two years she had changed her bigotry and uncharitable belief, for a faith in an Universal God, who is amply able to take care of his children, and gave her testimony, by being sprinkled, and joined the Universalist Church in Salem.

Near, or about this time, (1851,) I became conscious of some one rapping around me whenever I sat sewing or reading. I also found that an unusually chilly feeling accompanied these raps. I had heard my father, in my young days, tell about meeting his sister Belle, (spoken of in the first part of this work,) many times after she had passed from this earth, and she always seemed the same as in life, and that he always met her in the early morn, or late at night. I have heard him relate how he met her at four o'clock, on a bright summer morning, in the barn, as he went out to feed his cattle, she having been a braider of straw before passing away. She met him with a smile, and said, while swinging an unfinished hat in her hand, "Jesse, you have a man in your employ by the name of Runlet. Do you know any thing about his friends? He will die very soon. You had better attend to it at once."

We were then living at Sebasticook, Maine. At that time it was no easy task to travel many miles, as it was long before railroads in that part of the country, and stages were few and far between. My father questioned Mr. Runlet on the following day, concerning his friends, and found out where they lived. In two weeks Mr. Runlet died with typhus fever. But for the warning given my father by his spirit sister, he would not have known where to notify his friends, or who they were. I write this to show that my mediumistic powers come by inheritance, as well as through a peculiar organization; and also to assure the reader, that mediums are not made, but born. That is, that it is a gift, and grows with their growth, and cannot be acquired. That is the reason why there are so many counterfeits. But remember, there could never be a counterfeit, if there was not a genuine to copy from. I am obliged to refer often to my father, in this work, as I am not writing to please the fancy of my reader, but to establish a truth; and in so doing, I am in hopes to encourage my friends and readers — not to hide their gifts, under a bushel, but show them to the world, as God never gave any truly good gifts, unless intended for the benefit of humanity; and like the "Talents," spoken of by Him of old, will be called for in due time.

While I am relating some of my father's experiences, as told me by himself, I will also place here what may have been seen before by some, as I published it in the public press some years ago.

Some of my father's work, which he was advised to do under this same influence, was about forty-five years ago. His family were all passing away, member after member, with the old-fashioned consumption. Every two years there would be a vacant chair, until eight members of the family had gone to their long home, when Belle, (a sister) appeared to him, and told him to take up the one that died first, which was a sister, and burn her. It would put a stop to the ravages of the disease.

After many weeks of mental agony, and talking with my mother, and the earnest solicitations of his brother, who was then suffering from the dreadful disease, he had them taken up, and strange as it may seem, the one who died first, and had been dead sixteen years, — was found, upon opening the coffin, that the *clothing* and the body had all turned to a dark dust, but the lungs and heart were much larger than in a healthy human being. And there was evidence, that a strange and unknown law, had been at work, for on putting a lancet into the heart, the blood gushed forth as from a fresh wound.

Oh! you wise philosophers, why not learn that God speaks through His angels, to the children of men, and may convey this knowledge through the weak ones of earth to confound the wise. Surgeons and scientists would do well to become acquainted with this law, and not perform surgical operations, except in cases of necessity, without consulting the planetary law that rules every particle of life, and the life-principle in every thing. Experience and observation have taught me that no surgical operation should be performed on the increase of the moon. Cancers will grow, tonsils will come again, limbs will not heal, and there will be a return of the disease, if you trifle with it on the increase of the moon.

As man cannot govern the tides and the moon does, bow in reverence, all ye sages and saints, who hold scalpel and knife, and you will save many that now pass over in defiance of law. Man should never be forgetful of the law that controls him, or the God that rules him. It is that same law, that my father tried to understand, and obeyed in the burning of the bodies of those that had already passed away, that left our family free from consumption, from that time to the present, forty-five years.

As I am relating these peculiar incidents, I will here speak of something which happened to myself, when about seven years old; I was playing with my sister, and we wanted to fix a box by cutting off the cover. I ran and got a new hatchet that father had hidden from my brother, for fear he would get it and cut himself, not thinking we girls might use it. My sister took the hatchet and went to cut the cover, I holding it; she not only cut the box cover but took two of my fingers off also. I mention this to show that there is even in a child of seven years, intuitions that should be remembered. After the hand had been dressed by my father and mother, and the fingers placed in a box, they were buried. I can well remember, that they felt as if some one was squeezing my hand and fingers, and when the pain became unbearable, I begged my mother to give me my fingers, saying some one was hurting them. And after some coaxing, my father went and got them, and brought them to me; when lo, and behold, they were wrapped in a piece of flannel — which was rolled tightly around them. After separating them, and placing them in two different pieces, and laying something between them, they were put in a box and buried. The pain ceased, and I well remember the wonder it caused in my family; but I believe the same guides that assist me now, watched over me then.

Since that time, in my profession as a physician, I have seen men who have had their limbs amputated, who, on the full of the moon, would suffer extremely with pain, in the limb that had been removed years before; and I believe it is connected with the spiritual part of the human being, teaching us that there is a spiritual body, so in sympathy with the physical, that only death can break the tie. I was at one time obliged to visit a patient every month, and give him medicine to act upon the nerves of the brain and place a plaster on the spinal column, to relieve the distress in a limb which had been amputated seven years before.

Nothing a mystery is, but ignorance of the law. So we, like doubting Thomas, believed not, until he saw the very hands pierced by the nails, the wound thrust in the side, did he believe that Christ had risen, or He had "even" died.

Some ten years ago, while crossing the East Boston Ferry, a lady on the boat spoke to me, and asked me if I was Mrs. C——, the lady physician. I said, yes.

She said: "I am a stranger, but was told by my spirit mother to come and see you. I knew you as soon as I saw you. My mother has been with me three weeks, and advises me to return to my grandmother in New York state, that I may have proper care, in my last sickness; as I have been very much neglected by my husband. My spirit mother tells me to tell you concerning my sad life, as I do not expect to live long." I gave her my sympathy; she returned to her early home. I corresponded with her some months, when she passed away. The day she died, she received a letter from me, had the nurse read it to her and dictated an answer. The next morning, at four o'clock, I heard my name called; arose, and went into the entry. A cold draft of air came upon me, and a voice said, "I died yesterday at five o'clock, P. M. I send your letters and some other things in a package." In a few days I received a letter from the nurse, stating the hour of her death; also received the package in four weeks, containing my letters. The daughter of this lady is living, and can verify what I write.

Coming from Salem one day in the steam cars, we were very much crowded for room. A strange lady sat in the seat with me, and a gentleman and lady in front of us. I was reading a paper, when some one put their arms about my neck. It seemed so real, I mentally asked, "Who is this?" The person said,

"I am that gentleman's mother who sits in front of you." I said, "I cannot speak to him. You must call his attention to me, by touching him on the left side of his head." Soon he put up his hand and rubbed the left side of his head. I then said touch him on the right side. He put his hand up same as before, on the other side. I then told her to touch him on the sensorium. He lifted his hat, rubbed his head, and looked round at me. I paid particular attention to my paper, although I wanted to laugh. I asked what she wished to say to him. "Tell him not to sign that contract, to-day," she replied. When we arrived in Boston, I walked out of the Maine depot, and before I reached Hanover Street, the gentleman came up to me, lifting his hat, said, "will you please to excuse me, madam. Did you touch me in the car?" I said, "no, but I know who did. A lady who said she died three years ago, and is your mother. And says, "Edward, don't sign that contract, to-day." He was astonished, and I left him standing on the street pale and breathless. I moved on. I do not know who he was.

CHAPTER V.

From my seventh year, I became conscious of something seeming to have a care over me, some undefined presence, which I could feel, and yet could not express myself about it. At school it seemed easy to learn my lessons; if I wished to be at the head of my class, there seemed always something making me feel that if I tried, I would succeed. And in every way, even my most simple wish, seemed at times to be granted in my inner life. No disappointments seemed to wreck me, or affect me, because of that something, with its soothing influence, which always acted as a comforter. As time wore on, at about my sixteenth year, I began to feel as if my brain was so active, that it was almost impossible for me to contain myself, — so many queer sayings would come into my mind; and many times I have risen from my bed, when all were sleeping, to write prose and poetry, to relieve my aching head. Page after page would I write, and then commit to the flames next morning, saying I was nervous. Oh! how many aches and pains and mental agonies, are excused, or passed by, or accounted for, by that one *incomprehensible* word, nervousness. Would that it might be left out of the English language, and we put in some word more expressive of sympathy; for how many hearts are broken, how many brains gone mad, while nervousness, the only known expression serves to cover the ignorance of the law of inspiration or aspiration, and call it disease, that acts upon the bump of ideality.

Great heavens! do we not need the gateway of spirituality opened, to send down upon us poor mortals more sympathy and harmony? Is it not time that the Christ-principle was taught, and not only taught, but practiced, in this the nineteenth century? And that fathers and mothers should better understand the children they have been the means of bringing into the world,—and brothers and sisters try to see each other's inner life.

Look for the divinity that is within, instead of the faults from without. Instead of as to-day, part of a family living in extravagance and luxury, and other members of the same family, doing equally as much good in life, are struggling for a mere pittance, barely enough to keep soul and body together. Does any one believe God ordered all this? Ah! no, but the ruling of the planets, may be the cause of the innocent suffering for the guilty, and that may have something to do with the destinies of the human race.

If so, where is the blame, for there is one great

truth we all can understand, that we are placed here simply to grow, physically, morally, mentally, intellectually, and spiritually; and they who having the stronger spirituality, will in no wise be uncharitable to any of God's children, but what they do not understand, will leave for a time, when we shall all know what life and its sufferings mean.

It seems that the masses do not understand, that what we should most desire is growth, to fit ourselves to enjoy life, here and hereafter. It is not necessary to tell God what we need. He knows that already. But to return thanks is just, and gives us a renewal of spiritual inspirations, and makes us remember our weaknesses as human beings.

CHAPTER VI.

At nineteen years of age, I came to Boston to begin life, with new hopes and lofty ideas, as many a young girl leaves her home and friends, with a partner she has chosen from all others, to walk the pathway of life with. Ignorant and innocent, having been surrounded by religious influence at home, is it strange, that even to-day, while I write, a shudder passes over me, as I think of all the sorrows and disappointments that met me in my new home. All the pleasant imaginations of love and home, with its harmonies, took flight, and I found myself wrecked on the shoals of disappointment, where every young girl will find herself, if she does not wed principle and purity, for nature is always true to herself; and innocence can no more join hands with vice, than water can mix with oil. No matter how much deception is used, or how well selfishness may succeed, for a while, nature will rebel in due time; and though it may be many long weary years, that a patient husband or wife bear the cross, burdened at every step, yet there will come a time, when justice and truth will have their sway, and the selfish and deceitful will have it meted out to them, as they have measured it to others.

Then; and not until then, when disappointment had nearly wrecked my life, and I had been pronounced a consumptive by the wise but mistaken physicians, I felt how near, and yet how far, were those unseen ones, who cheered me in my loneliness, and held me up when I would have fallen, guided and directed me by their intuitive instruction, yet I had not received any open demonstration from them; still, in my soul, when sorrow reached my spirit, I would feel their warm breath on my face, and their loving sympathy in my soul, and hear the whispered words, *be brave.* Oh! how in my disappointed life, when I felt it was more than I could bear, have I thrown my arms out into space, trying to catch, or feel a touch of those, who though unseen, lived and loved me still. The religious element in my nature, would rise up in my daily life, and on bending knees, would I plead to God to spare my unborn child the consequent effects of an inharmonious marriage, though entered into in ignorance and girlish innocence. And I believe my prayers were taken up by the angelic hosts, and carried to my Master, who answered my prayers, willingly; and the daughter, who blesses my life to-day with her heavenly gifts, is an assurance of God's love and tenderness to his children. Oh! woman, you who read this little book, may it bring to your soul a balm, to know that there is one woman amidst the millions who dared to suffer and be strong, and wait God's own time, to be emancipated from deceptive surroundings. Let it give you strength to bear the ills of life, but work in some good cause, and help those weaker than yourself. It is the only balm for a disappointed life, to fulfill one's duties, and help others that we may be happy ourselves. And, mothers, looking back thirty years, it seems but yesterday, when placed in my arms was my first child; no one but a mother, whose love is centered on her child, by disappointment, can realize my joy at beholding the tiny form of my darling child, with its innocent face, teaching me that there was something in life worth living for. To watch and care for my helpless little one, revived in my inner being, the true elements of the true woman,—love for innocence and helplessness. We may have everything in life that money can bring, but the loving word mother, may well repay us for many of life's disappointments, and also bring out of a lonely heart, feelings of responsibility and care, that makes up the true and noble woman. I was not conscious of any person around me, until some time afterwards, when my second child was thirteen months old, when I was aroused, while quietly sleeping, one night, *to hear the words*, "make lots of night dresses, for baby's going to be long sick, and you will need them; then he comes to summer land."

Somewhat dejected in spirit, feeling that something was going to happen, I went busily to work and made the night dresses, as was commanded me to do. This was the first of July, he was taken sick soon after, and passed away October eighth. The day before he was taken sick, my little daughter was learning her Catechism for Sunday School, and laying her head in my lap, while Georgie was sitting up in his cradle, she said, "Mother, where is God? I don't see Him." Georgie looked up, and with a sweet smile said, raising his little hands, "God is up there." I was startled, as he had never spoken a word, but pa and mamma; and in my surprise, said, "Georgie, did you speak?" when he reiterated the same sentence to me again, with so much solemnity, that it fairly chilled me, and when my husband returned at night, he found me very much depressed in mind, and as is usual in such cases, called it nervousness, and told me to go out for a walk, as being with the children so much, affected me. I went, and when I returned, found my darling sick; and after nine week's sickness he passed to the summer land. I sincerly believe that children grow up spiritually beside their earthly mother, learning earth's laws, in connection with spirit; and my reason for this is, that for many years, at times I was conscious of the name of mother being whispered in my ear. At times I was very lonely and sad, and sometimes would weep, missing him, and also another I had lost since he passed away, — when I beheld him, standing before me one evening, and he seemed like a child four or five years old. He said, "don't cry, mamma, for me; we are always near you. See," and he held up his little dress, when lo! and behold, it was wet and clung about him; and he said, "mamma, your tears make my dress wet. I can't sleep good, if you cry." I was astonished, and said, "is it possible, darling, that mother's troubles affect you so?" and he passed from my sight. But I learned a lesson from that, to do my duty by every one while they live, and when they have passed on, leave them in the hands of a Higher power. But I feel that the law of attraction between the spirit of mother and child, must be as strong, spiritually, as physically, — laws which have been proven to hold good in the transmission of disease from both parents to their children.

Three years after Georgie's death, we buried another little boy, with disease of the brain; and as I looked on his waxen features, I began to ask myself the question, why this disease of the brain should affect my children, both in the same way, and at about the same age; and if there was not some law which I had transgressed unknowingly. As I was of a studious turn of mind, and believed in physiology and phrenology, I at once set about trying to solve the problem concerning the death of those loved ones. And I feel to-day, that I can safely attribute it to a weak physical body, and a too strong mental action of the mother; and that while my children were blessed with strong spirituality and mental power, there was not physical strength, inherited from their mother, to sustain them in physical life, and then we are taught that God takes our children away. Be that true or false, I learned a lesson in the death of my little ones, that satisfied me that they partoook of the weak physical nature of the mother; for the two children who resemble their father, are living; while those resembling their mother have been denied their just rights of living their allotted time on the earth, by the injustice and disappointment meted out to their mother.

I give this here, that mothers may help me solve this momentous question, why so many children pass away in infancy, and are denied their just rights of a life on the physical plain. I can safely say it is due to prenatal conditions, and inharmonious surroundings, and ignorant physicians, which cheat these little innocents out of a true life, and oblige them, in spirit, to walk side by side with their mother, and through her life, to be made acquainted with physical law. If not so, no individuality could come to them; and so, mothers, when you think it is better for your darling to pass away in infancy, first think what they were placed here for, and you will not be hypocrite enough to believe that it is as well for them.

But, mothers, look beyond the tomb,
And see thy little ones,
Protected by the Friend, who says,
Oh! suffer such to come.

CHAPTER VII.

"STAR-MAY."

As years wore on, I still seemed to be watched by unseen beings, and whispering voices seemed to attend me, when, being suddenly awakened from my sleep one night, I was told to get up; and I beheld a dark face bending over me, with long black hair falling about the shoulders, and a piece of red cloth folded about the person. I arose, when a voice said, "remove the woolen carpet from the floor. Pack away your feather beds, and all unnecessary clothing; get an open stove and a tin tea-kettle, for you will need them. Brave is going to have the small pox. Boil tar in the water to purify the air, and say nothing." I was astounded, and who would not have been? for in 1855 we were not used to the small pox, as we are at the present, and it seemed a very loathsome disease. It was Wednesday night. The face glided by me with a sweet smile, as if it only meant me kindness. The next morning I did as directed, replaced the woolen carpet with a straw matting, procured a stove and kettle, and the tar; and when my husband returned at night, he complained of a bad head-ache, and insisted upon having a sweat, which was given him. At twelve o'clock that night, my name was called again, when I beheld the same face saying, "get up, your husband will be broken out with small pox before morning." I arose, and lifting the wet cloth I had placed on his forehead, found him all broken out. Sending for a physician in the morning, he pronounced it small pox at once. My husband, for three weeks, was very sick, when my little daughter was taken with the same dread disease, and lay very sick.

The day it turned with him he was suffering very much; and I, worn out with care and watching, being forsaken by every one, they were so frightened of it, and the physician only stepped into the door, never into his room, and I had not seen the face of any one since they were taken sick,—only the doctor for a moment. Disheartened and discouraged, I felt a fearful head-ache coming on me, and the chill they both complained of when taken, and knowing we all must suffer if I should be taken down with it, and knowing how unfeeling my neighbors had shown themselves in their fright, (for they even complained because I opened my windows at night to air the house,) I expected no help from that source; and we all know how little avail human sympathy, when they think there is danger to themselves. My husband insisted upon having something to make him sleep; he did not care what it done to him, his sufferings were so great.

As I passed down the stairs to get something for him, the little brown face smilingly said, "be quick, squaw, empty the laudinum into a cup, fill the bottle with black tea. Give Brave some; he will sleep." I hurried to do so, feeling God had sent some one to me in my helplessness and loneliness; and feeling so sick myself, that after I had administered the tea, I came down stairs, fell on my knees, and with my soul full of thankfulness, uttered these words:—"*God, help me!*" A hand was laid upon my head, and I heard the words:—"*Fear not, my child.*" I arose from my knees, so happy, that a sweet melody filled my soul, and I burst forth, and sang as in my happiest days, when my father played the bass viol, and taught his children to rise and fall the notes.

Oh! you faithless ones, that do not believe in answer to prayer. When you feel your own weakness, and have no confidence in human aid, and your spirit needs to be strengthened, believe me, there is a fountain which will never fail us, and when you once drink from that fountain, you can never thirst. For that fountain is Inspiration, and Intuition, and spirits of loved ones, are always watching and waiting, to carry our wants and wishes up higher, and bring the balm of Gilead. to our weary and waiting souls.

Strange as it may seem, the tea given to my husband for laudinum, had the desired effect to promote sleep, and feeling that he was laboring under a narcotic, so affected him, that he slept all night, and the next morning was decidedly better, and in due time both recovered their usual health.

CHAPTER VIII.

From 1850 to 1860, my health seemed to fail slowly but surely; and at last I became so reduced, that after consulting many physicians, it was decided that I was in consumption; and there are now living, (1881) physicians who decided that my left lung was entirely gone. I weighed only eighty pounds, and for three years had not been able to lie on either side.

Life seemed almost a burden, — I constantly trying to be busy, to keep my mind from destroying me, with constant thinking, knowing I could not live long with my left lung gone, and the right one in a diseased condition. I continued to decline, and after a time began spitting blood. My attendant physician said I must soon pass away.

I, feeling no doubt like many young persons under such circumstances, as if I was being dealt unjustly with, became rebellious in my feelings, asking myself why was I placed in such circumstances. It was nothing I had done myself,, and if it was because of my innocence and ignorance, why had not God taught the children of earth, the why and wherefore of life?

I had not the least fear of death, but I wanted to know why God did not give us the information we sought, and make us realize what was expected of us. I was not hypocrite enough to say I was thankful to be brought into life, without any volition of my own, have my early hopes blasted by circumstances, and then bow like a whipped cur, and say I believe it right!

Not so. If God, is a God of love and wisdom, He will accept no such hypocritical worship. And if He desired to be worshipped in spirit and in truth, He could not receive worship from a child, who could say with the lips that it was right, and rebel in their innermost soul. I have yet to see the man or woman, (and I have stood beside many death-beds), that have not lived their allotted time, and are aged, but ask the same question,—why are we put here to suffer so much, and told so little. Only, that it is God's will, and we must submit without a murmur. The very men and women that preach such doctrine, should be obliged to bring proof, and prove it in public, or be placed with false teachers.

What right has any one, man or woman, to put forth to the world, theological views, as facts, which cannot be proven only through a record three thousand three hundred years old, lost for four hundred years, brought to light by the Mohammedans, acknowledged by Christians, to be written by men inspired of God, to do the work, just as some are (inspired) to-day, which that same class of theologians reject as being inspired by demons, — and that record only one side of the question, giving only the history of the Jews? We of the class called Gentiles, afterwards Christians, could come and tell you concerning the Holy Nazerene, — as told us by the Magi of Persia, or the Egyptian priest, whom Jesus learned his lessons of wisdom with; and knowing that He was sent to set an example for the nations to follow, revered Him as the Messiah, whom God had sent not to bear all the terrible wrong doing of a wicked people, but to teach them to love one another, and not allow selfishness and avariciousness to destroy the God-like principle, *love*, that is inherent in them. Not that we are saved by His death, but by His life and example, — and I believe, had I loved God less, and feared Him more, I should not be here writing these words to-day. But I believed Him to be a God of love and wisdom, and felt in my weakness that He who placed me here, would answer me, if I asked Him, in spirit and in truth. And I asked in sincerity, that if I must pass away so young, (only twenty-nine years old), I might have given me the reason. Yes, even more, I demanded it, as my right as a child of God, who had no fear of a loving Father, only love for Him. We are taught He is more loving than an earthly parent. Prove it, ye faithless ones, and not talk what you do not believe.

God heard my request, and through His ministering angels answered my prayer of demand; and I would not exchange the knowledge for all the gold on our earthly plain, for that will pass away, but that knowledge will be the key which unlocks all the mysteries of human life.

I retired as usual one night, when I felt a chilly feeling pervade the atmosphere of my room, and looking up, beheld what appeared to be a smoking substance, arising from the floor to the ceiling. I watched it, and as a numbness crept over me, I said, "why, perhaps this is a feeling of death." But as I watched, the face of my father came out of it, and he said, "you have made a demand upon spirit life, my child, and God has sent me to answer it; but you are aware, that if we restore you to health, you must give us something in return." I said, "I have nothing to give, father." He said, "I am not all who have suffered in answer to your demand. The world you live in, is a world of demand, and the spirit world, is a world of supply to your souls; but, there must be an exchange of life, if we answer your petition." He said, "there are fifty or more who compose a band; what will you give them to live, and work out a life of usefulness?" I answered, "I have nothing." He said, "will you dedicate yourself to the *human race, and be guided* as a physician and *worker* in every good cause, whatsoever you are told to do for the good of the children of earth?" I said, "*I will*,"—but said he, "that will not do. Repeat after me these words: 'I, Julia A. Norcross, dedicate myself to any good work, which shall be given me to do, by my angel guides, while life lasts. I will not fail in that work, so help me God, and my Angelic Band.'"

Then he said, "I shall never come again this way, but you will always be told what to do, and how. You will also be protected by your guides. Go fearlessly along, turn not to the right, or to the left. Whatever obstruction comes in the way, to interfere in any good work, will be removed. Be charitable, kind and loving to all, and forget not your promise, and you shall be blessed; you will suffer much, but that will be nothing. The world will not understand a truth, unless there are martyrs to every good cause. Cross your hands upon your chest, and also cross your feet at ten o'clock every forenoon, and four every afternoon. You will then feel the Hand healing you, and teaching you to care for yourself. You will see written that which will cure you, and when you have cured yourself, you will extend the hand of healing to others, and by doing so you will strengthen yourself. You will always feel the Hidden Hand on your shoulder, and will know we are some of us near. *Talk to us as if you saw us;* we will advise you, as you will never be where we cannot come to you."

And amidst all the ups and downs of life, I have been guided and guarded, by that Hidden Hand,—and chided, if need be. It always accompanies me, wherever I go; and at times, when visiting my patients late at night, when it would come into my mind how late it was, and I out alone, I would feel the Hand upon my shoulder, as much as to say, *never alone.* And while life lasts, and I remain a sojourner on earth plain, I shall be, as I always have been, true to the band that guides me, feeling assured that God knew it was best, for the thorns to wound my feet, and disappointment blast my young life; that out of the ashes of the past, might be resurrected a hand to heal, a psychological power to assist, and a sympathetic feeling to encourage the sick and suffering. And if humble me, has been chosen, I can do no more than submit to a power Higher than myself, and wait the coming of the glorious morn of spirit life. To understand why it has been so with me, and why we who are chosen should suffer scoff and scorn, and by those who are linked to us by the tenderest ties that can possibly unite human beings, and even the sacredness of consanguinious relationship, is not exempt from acting its part in withholding from us sympathy and encouragement,—but when angel hosts attend our footsteps, and faith inspires our soul, we can bide our time, and wait the coming light, for life is short, and eternity is long; and perhaps we shall all understand one another better. If my cross has been hard to bear, I know many times I have made it lighter, by helping others to bear their sufferings and cares; and then when I have sighed, in the hours of trouble, and felt that only a thin veil had been drawn between me, and those I loved, in spirit, and I was tired and weary of the turmoil of life, I would beg of them to open the gateway and give me a glimpse of the higher life. I have been answered, "be brave; all things are for the best."

Why murmur, when you cannot change
  Conditions, over which you have no control;
Arise, let circumstances flee,
  But do not bind thy eternal soul;
For if the life that makes you mourn,
  Or sadness follows in the way,
Look thou to higher realms above, —
  You'll see the clouds all roll away.

So, weary sister, live and hope,
  That by-and-by, duties, well done,
Will come and bring their recompense,
  And you'll be blessed for every one.
Bear now the cross, the end is near;
  Thy trials cannot weigh thee down;
For we have watched thee in the past,
  And thou shalt wear life's peaceful crown.

Keep up thy spirits, let nothing crush
  Thy mental powers, nor make them change,
For all but life, must go to dust,
  And by God's laws must be arranged;
Seek those that give thee mental strength,
  So that thy lamp may brightly burn;
And if thou needst love's eloquence,
  God gives to them, that rightly earn.

Do that which makes thee safe and strong,
  And gird thyself with fearless might;
And love no one, if they would wean
  Thy loving soul from what is right.
If they who come and ask thy love,
  And cannot pay the precious dower,
You might as well be left alone,
  As give thyself into their power.

If thou art tired, weary and weak,
  Not to such fountains shouldst thou drink;
For when thy strength exhausted be,
  Their weight would only make thee sink.

CHAPTER IX.

My health improved rapidly, and I found myself a new being, physically; and as I improved in health, my mental seemed to be acted upon in a very singular manner, and I gave attention to it. There would be a strange feeling come on the right side of my brain, which I learned was the positive side; and information would be conveyed to me, on the left, which is the negative side; and whatever they wished me to do, has been given me in that way. And when I feel the Hidden Hand upon the right side, *I know it is to give me instruction.* And when I feel a touch on the left shoulder, it is some one wanting information. When on the sensorium, it incites the spiritual and intellectual. But I have no desire to impress upon my readers that this is an easy way to get an education. Let me assure you, that no great blessing ever comes to earth's children without sorrow and suffering attending every step. No proclamation of emancipation ever came to the children of men, only through sorrow and bloodshed, and hours of agony and despair.

The Hidden Hand was my solace and comforter, and my spirit was made glad by the restoration of my physical body to health, giving me more physical force and stamina, to withstand the opposition and ridicule which the ignorant and malicious will always bring forth against any thing which they do not understand, and are too indolent and worldly to wish too. · Bear in mind that they, too, shall have their reward; for whatsoever they have "meted to others, shall be meted to them again."

This year, 1861, there came to my home another son, and for two years my time was taken up with my domestic affairs; but still my guides watched me carefully and were constantly about me, and often surprised me by some peculiar act to assure me of their power and protection,—one instance of which I will here relate. I asked my husband, one Saturday evening, to bring me a half-dozen glass goblets; and to annoy me, and also to ridicule my temperance principles, he brought me in six common bar-tumblers. I was vexed, but said nothing. On setting my table Sunday evening for Monday morning breakfast, I placed three of those tumblers on each end of the table, and went into my sitting room. Presently I heard a noise, as if some one striking on glass with a piece of metal; I went into the dining-room, and found one of the tumblers cut off about an inch from the bottom, and a knife laying beside it. Suffice it to say, that before Monday night, all the half-dozen were destroyed in the same manner.

An Indian girl (spirit,) calling herself "Star-May," said "she had done it to let Brave know that she knew what was right and what was wrong."

At this time the spirits gave Mr. C. a prophetic warning: saying if he was not kind to his wife and children, there would be a time when she would stand upon a public rostrum, and he in the audience, when the Atlantic ocean might as well roll between. And to-day, after all these years have past, I can see how well it has all been fulfilled; and if coming events cast their shadows before, does it not imply that our acts have to do with our destiny?

CHAPTER X.

In 1863 my mediumistic work began in earnest. In January I was at Mr. D. S——'s, and while sitting around a table with some friends, was conscious of being controlled or influenced in a mysterious way; was told I had offered an invocation, which proof I had by finding my face and eyes much swollen the following morning, which disappeared towards evening, and the next evening another invocation, with the same results. This lasted about twelve days, with no conversation through me upon any subject.

Then came what purported to be the spirit of Dr. Kittridge, and made himself known through me, telling me what I must do, was to examine diseases, and use the hand of healing. For six months I examined all diseases free of charge; and in that year examined over six hundred persons, and wrote prescriptions, and gave such advice as their cases called for; after which my spirit guides suggested that I put up my own medicine, as my magnetism would impregnate it, and it would have better effect upon the system. About this time I was called to Mr. G. L——d, who had been sick a number of years, with what was called by the physicians, neuralgia of the stomach. He had even been to California, to try the effects of climate, yet to no purpose. When I was called, he was suffering from an acute attack, was attended by *two* physicians, who had blistered and salivated him, all to no purpose; then tried rolling him on a mattress. His wife, (Mrs. S. A. L——d), having heard of the power recently bestowed on me, determined to try this wonderful gift of healing. Although a stranger and a skeptic, she sent for me about eight o'clock, P. M. As soon as I entered the room, I became influenced at once, and bade him arise from the mattress and go to bed. His wife said it was impossible, he could not move; when I reached out my hand, and raised him at once, and led him to his room, his wife putting him in bed. Seating myself at the bed-side, I took his hand in mine, placing the other on his forehead, remained under influence till five o'clock the next morning, he sleeping, and waking entirely free from pain; my guides deciding that it was gall stones passing through the gall duct, and inflammation of the liver. It caused me more trouble to cure the effects of the calomel which the other physicians had given him, than to cure the effects of the disease; although having been subject to like attacks for fifteen years, he never had a return of it afterwards.

After several years of health and happiness, Mr. L——d met with an accident on the Metropolitan Railroad, which disabled him for life, and finally caused his death. In a suit for damages against the railroad, I was called as a witness in his behalf, before a bench of judges, opposed by three of our most eminent and able lawyers, one of whom has since filled the governor's chair in this State: and could they behold their littleness in comparison with those whose hand turned the scale in favor of the poor and unfortunate man who laid helpless for two years on a bed of suffering, and a rich corporation, trying to shirk the responsibility, and fighting against justice and mercy, for a few paltry dollars, which will hang like a mill-stone about their necks, after they have left this earth to render an account, and have their case decided according to the laws of the spirit world, where justice, mercy and truth abound.

Not one question was asked me while on the stand, in favor of that poor man, but an answer was whispered to me, in my ear, from outside of myself, by the angel hosts, showing me how interested the spirit influences were, concerning the troubles and afflictions of earth's children, and also teaching me that it is not the influential, but the upright, that God sends His messengers to attend; and if those men were aware that their thoughts and purposes were pre-arranged by an unseen power, they would not have tried so hard to rob a poor injured man, by twisting the law, for oftentimes there is more law than justice. But I beheld the working of that unseen power, and it was only through the influence that was thrown over the judges, by a power not recognized by themselves, that they did at last give justice.

I saw a spirit recording the thoughts, as they came from each man's brain, and giving him due credit *for only that* which came from his own inner life; and then using the manipulations of a magnetic power to change his mind. But of that he gained no reward. Oh! how little in comparison with those workers, was the talk and mean insinuations thrown out by those lawyers, to prove the witnesses' statements false. Judges and lawyers should remember, that there is a higher law than that made by man; and as they are only men, they should, if they accept such responsible situations from the people, conduct themselves in such a manner, that the unseen police, who never receives bribes, nor sleep at their post, may send in their report to head-quarters in their favor;— for believe me, every act of yours is seed sown, and in due time you will reap the harvest, *nolens volens.*

A little circumstance connected with this case, may be interesting to our readers, as all I shall write in this book is true, and can be vouched for, by those in my own vicinity.

Mr. L—— having been sick a long time, many

called upon him, because his case was a sad one; one of whom was lawyer B——. He said his sympathy was so great, that it gave him pain to see him suffer so, and asked Mr. L—— what he could do for him. In reply he said, I have many bills out, (Mr. L—— having been in the grocery business previous to his injury), and am in need of money; asked him if he would collect some of them. Lawyer B—— said he would, on a very small commission. Mr. L—— gave him some bills for collection, of which he collected fourteen dollars, and kept the money. And after Mr. L—— died, sued the widow for four hundred dollars, as fees, for services in assisting her husband in his business.

Is it any wonder that people who see a church with such a wolf within its folds, should say that ill-gotten money is paid in to retain a place, and that church must get some of the dirt that such a man carries into it. Brothers and sisters, overcome evil with good, is God's law, and not to let evil overcome good, and make everything evil. Too many of God's children are judged by what they wear, and churches are not exempt from its fearful influence in this direction.

CHAPTER XI.

Continuing my practice, and attending to my family, gave me very little time for social intercourse with any society, and I saw, as all physicians do, so much of suffering, both physical and mental; for it is not only the body that a true physician is obliged to prescribe for, but many of the ills that belong to the mental; and sometimes all the troubles of a family are deposited with the family physician; and if he or she is false to their trust, they are no physician, in the true sense of the word.

At this time I was called to a Mr. N., who had not seen a well day for ten years. His last physician had tried all kinds of experiments upon him, and then told him he would never be any better. He had a very singular dream. In it he saw a lady that held a bottle towards him, and on it these words: — "*Behold I come to bring relief!*" He being a man of strong will-power, and not to be laughed out of what to him seemed so real in his dream, he sent for many lady physicians, but to no purpose; he would say that is not the one. At last some one was in his house telling that there was a lady on Brooks Street, East Boston, who had just begun to practice, and I was sent for. As soon as he saw me, he said, this is the one I saw in my dream. I shall be cured. He was very much reduced, thin and weak, but of a will that was wonderful. He engaged me at once, stipulating a sum I should receive every Saturday evening, and also agreeing that he would do whatever my guides saw fit for him. And I will here state that I never had a patient that showed more fortitude in suffering, or more faith in the influence which he could not see, but so easily feel. Oftentimes I would sit by the bed, and his wife a little distance from me, when I would feel the power taken from my brain, and conveyed to his, and in a few minutes he would be sleeping soundly. We would leave the room, and he would sleep till morning. This was all the opiate he received during my three month's treatment of him; the guides telling him he was so weak, they could magnetize him through me, as it was conducive to his cure, — he had taken so much poisonous medicine before.

While I attended him, all his medicines were prepared by myself, and his wife, from instructions through me, by my spirit guides. And in three months from the time I was first called to him, he was a well man, and for fourteen years enjoyed good health, and gave to the world the truths he had learned, while lying upon a bed of suffering, — that there were spirit guides, interested in earthly scenes, and that they could manifest themselves through human organizations.

Who can tell why such changes take place in the circumstances that surround human beings? At the time I attended Mr. N——, his minister, for he belonged to the Methodist church, used to come quite often to see him, and became very much interested in his case, and gleaned all the information he could concerning his cure; and many times, on a Sunday morning, when reading to, or praying with my patient, would this man stand outside in the hall, waiting to be admitted. He seemed surprised, that we who held spiritual views should offer prayer. Why, the word Spiritualism itself, implies intercourse with the departed, and a positive belief in a future existence; and prayer is the sincere desire of the heart, flowing out towards the great source of all purity and life, God, or an outflow of the divinity within us. And no person, understanding spiritual truth, could fail to see that to own our being influenced or controlled by those in spirit life, who had lived and suffered, whose love and sympathy were with us, who had been praying spirits, or those who had devotion large in their own physical organization, but would offer prayer to the Giver of all good.

I attended in the family at times for fourteen years,

when, on returning from a journey, I was told that he, Mr. N., was very sick, and had sent for me, having been sick three weeks. I hastened to his bedside, and never shall I forget the agonizing face that looked up into mine. After I had made an examination, he asked, "What do you think ails me?" I said, "typhoid, gastric fever." "Well," said he, "I shall then die; and I think my doctor had better be in the country, digging potatoes, than to be here practicing medicine. He never got a living at preaching, and so took up doctoring. I waited for you, and this is the result. He has been treating me for simple diarrhœa, and I have felt that I was very sick." In a few days he passed away.

Strange to say, that was the same man, that fourteen years before was a preacher. God did not elect him for the work. So he is to-day doing worse, trifling with the bodies of human beings, without the least adaption for the work, not knowing that surely he will reap his reward.

CHAPTER XII.

Those who do not understand spirit influence, may be glad to learn how a new influence approaches a medium.

1st. By throwing upon the physical body of the medium, the symptoms of the disease they had before they passed away. 2d. By touch or influence on the left or negative side. 3d. By a blending of the mental, or spiritual, through the law of attraction. Such medium cannot be controlled for physical manifestations, or materializations. For the mystery of mediumship, is the mystery of human life itself, and depends almost wholly upon inherited temperaments, peculiar organization, original gifts, and careful culture. It is not really necessary one should be entranced to receive communications from the spirit world, or to get impressions, or even give tests. Often, conscious-mediums are the most reliable. Sometimes, when persons enter my office, they bring with them their spirit friends, and these spirit friends come up to me, and blend so easily with me, that for the time being, I seem to be the person themselves, and can go on and tell precisely what they wish to say, and know and feel, that the spirit stands at my side; and I feel the influence upon my face, and for the time, we are one, blending our spirits; and yet I am conscious, all of the time, and conversing with persons in the room, at the same time. But it would be impossible for me to do this of my own will, or by appointment, or for money, let the amount be ever so great. In these communications I have never known one word to be false; but when communications are given by guides, they are sometimes mistaken in what they relate, showing that they do not see clearly, and I have proven it in more instances than one.

In January, 1874, I entered Music Hall, Boston, to hear Gerald Massay lecture, and when seated, a strange lady came and seated herself beside me. My eyes closed without volition of my own, and I seemed to be another person. A spirit said to me, help me to reach my mother. I turned to the lady, and told her a brother of hers, was standing beside me, — that he wanted to write to his mother. Neither of us had paper or pencil. I was obliged to send out for them. When they came, I wrote all the particulars concerning his mysterious death; and the reasons for it, which had ever been a mystery to them, — the sister sobbing all the while, — and the spirit keeping my eyes closed all the time, that I might not see what was written. Also gave her information concerning some work she was doing at her home. She was an entire stranger to me, I never having seen her before, neither have I since. Strange as it may seem, I was seemingly conscious all the while, and yet heard nothing of the lecture.

The lady was never in Boston before, and left that evening; next morning I received the following note:—

BOSTON, JAN., 11th, 1874.

MY DEAR MRS. CRAFTS:

As I have so very brief a time to stay, (we go at 8.30), I can say but a few words; but I do desire to thank you from my heart, for the comfort you have given me. May God bless you in your work. If you should again be influenced by the spirit who came to-day, I wish you would write me. Do not hesitate to tell me just what he says—let it be what it may. I think I shall see you again in this life, but if not, farewell, and God bless you.

Your friend,

E. L. K——.

CHAPTER XIII.

Cheered and comforted by outside influence, is the experience of every true medium, through the blending of the outside spirit, with our inner life; yet there may be doubting ones, as there always will be, but if they desire to solve this great problem, let them just examine themselves; as many will say to me, "why do I not have these things come to me?" But on acquaintance with them, I cease to wonder. The lack of spirituality, avariciousness, want of sincerity, selfishness, jealousy, uncharitableness, and a whole catalogue of minor evils, which they can see in others, are simply the reflection of what exists in themselves. Who, but themselves, know the sacrifices that poor mediums make, in fighting this battle for the emancipation of thought? I have always been busy with my own affairs, endeavoring to solve the reason why there was so much difference in the same family, although the same father and mother; and why there was so much love between some of the members of the same family, and so little between others. And I have come to this conclusion, that there is some truth, and a great deal of philosphy, in a planetary law, that in some way rules the events of life, which, in due time, will be given to the world, in a way easier to be understood than now; and it may explain why there is such a tendency for members of the same family to take up different opinions and professions, and go through life under certain circumstances, in spite of all opposition or censure to the contrary, and live out their own natural life. God speed the time when this opposition may cease, as persons are oftentimes on the verge of the grave, before justice is rendered them. As patients enter my office, I glance at them, and place them at once, under the planetary law, which I think they belong; and will say I have been astonished at the results, the similiarity of action and expression; and am convinced that if I had the time to spare, could make it one of the most pleasing of the natural sciences, that could be learned to an intelligent people; and I even now would not be associated in business, with man or woman, who had Mars governing the upper, and Saturn the lower part of the face, as experience has taught me very sad lessons in that direction. I am not writing to prove astrology, or fatalism, but believe there is something in the science; and the only way we can overcome the consequences of the planetary condition, is by the law of cultivation concerning every thing that pertains to life; and in so doing, we become receptive to the influences of the higher intelligences. I have asked the question many times of astrologists, and their answers would tend to make one a materialist, which I never could be; and I will answer my reader in my own way: —

In my young days I was fond of reading. In my more mature years, was an observer and thinker, and being blessed with an organization, or disposition, to naturally aspire to spiritual things. God has answered the aspirations of my soul, by giving me inspiration to act from. I cannot conceive how any man or woman, believing in God, and the immortality of the soul, can doubt spirit influences. For do we not all exercise more or less influence over one another? The positive will ever hold the negative in subjection. And do we not know that it is not the body, but the spirit and will, that exercises the power over those with whom we come in contact? And is there any thing strange, miraculous or irreligious, in the belief, that when we lay aside the human body, that the active, thinking spirit, with its own individuality, can be cognizant of those they have left in the body? And would it not be the most natural thing in the world for them to manifest to us, if they so desire? Does it look strange, to a sensible, thinking man or woman, that my father, dying away from home and his loved ones, should wish to make himself known? and would it not be the best way to come to his own child, (which I know he did,) and when he had learned that he could stand beside her, and through her sensitive nature, get an answer from her spirit to his, would it not be likely that such information would be improved upon? And when there are others that have gone into spirit life, is it any thing strange that they should wish to employ the same means to reach their friends? If any of us should visit another country, and there find a gold mine, enough for all our friends, and if love toward them filled our souls, should we not be likely to try and inform them, so that they might reap the benefit? I feel and believe that our departed friends, going to the spirit world, where they find the law of correspondence, and the law of compensation, to be a reality, would wish to make it known; would it not be natural for them to come to us, and tell us each in their own way, when they know that Heaven has only been a speculative question among us, as it has always been, too unreal a Heaven, and too miserable a Hell? I have talked with persons, who would work hard to disprove and believe, or accept, any hypothesis, however absurd, rather than accept the true, simple *truth*, of spirit communion. And if the New Testament does not teach spiritual communication, what does it teach? Oh! how much I have to thank God for, that no opposition, or censure, or inducement, could make me renounce *my* faith in the belief of spirit communion, and power of assistance, if we live up to the higher principles.

It is a source of the greatest pleasure to me, to know that my father, brothers, children and friends, do come and hold social converse with me, each in their own way; and nothing in life would I accept in exchange for this knowledge and privilege. Never in my life did I feel to be doing God's work more, than when a niece of mine came to me, and threw her influence upon me with such feelings of grief and sadness concerning her parents, saying her father was sick, and what would her mother do, if he should be taken from her? I said, "what can I do?" she said, "write to them or go; I can follow your vitality in the letter, and can see mother and father, while they read it, and I cannot without." I wrote to them, and in a few days she came to me, and threw upon me a similar grief; and though semi-conscious myself, could not prevent her talking and crying through me, and I gained some very queer information concerning that letter. After a time I determined to go myself. I took plenty of time, going over the house, saying nothing to any one, knowing that the dear child was using my eyes to see father, mother, brothers and sisters, and viewing the new home, (a new house they had recently moved into.) When I retired for the night, myself and husband talked by raps, until two o'clock in the morning, with the unseen ones. And my niece said, "you will tell grandmother that I can see her rooms also, and that Willie and I, with lots of others, have seen both the new homes. But they are not like our's; ours are so different." I asked, "in what way different?" She said, "I'm not permitted to tell all about it." "Are you satisfied?" I asked. "Oh! yes," was the reply; "and sometime I will tell you something, when you are where I can." Some months after, it had entirely gone from my mind, my husband and I stepped into a spiritual seance, where they were all strangers. The medium was a gentleman; he looked around to me and said, "there is some one here, that calls you, Julia, and said you were kind to send the box." I said, "thank you, for letting me know." "Never mind, *you've* done your duty, and God will bless you." He then said, "there is a young girl who says her name is Rosa, and she was named for her aunt Rosinia." I thanked her. There is no science so interesting to me as the spiritual, which teaches man and woman the responsibility resting upon them in regard to their duties in life, and towards others. Spiritualism may have attached to it many things that are objectionable, and need to be weeded out of its ranks. No sincere spiritualist but will admit that. But to say that all mediums are frauds, or dishonest, because they cannot explain the faith that is in them, or the wonderful things that come to them, is too much. (St

John, iii.: 8.) Can we expect it, when there has been so many mistakes made by great and good men, in every age? What theologian can give you any positive proof that his faith is a correct one? Can he demonstrate it beyond a doubt? If not then why condemn another for differing from him in opinion? Theologians have been the cause of the lack of harmony which exists in the religious world to-day, by reason of the selfishness of mankind, perverting the God-like principle *love*, which is, or should be the basis of all Christianity. Where is the man who dares to express his whole soul concerning the spirit world, if he belongs to any particular school of theology? So it is left to those who are untrammeled in their opinions, to open up this advanced science, and face the opposition, as education, in one line of thought or direction, tends to bigotry, and not advancement.

A person of religious sentiment, once said to me, there is one failure with you mediums, — you are too willing to give thanks to your spiritual guides, and forget God, the giver. That I never do; but if I pray to God, I would return thanks to those spirit guides, who are so tangible to me, whom I know to be my father and friends. (1, John, 4—20.)

I cannot believe that God who is everywhere and in everything, and perfect in his attributes, would come in contact with imperfect beings, and show a separate individuality from our own. For sometime, when we are influenced, the name of the controlling spirit is given at once. At one time I had a lady in my house, who was a medium, and we could sit together and hold a slate, and have it filled with writing, by unseen hands. Hundreds of messages were given that way, with names signed to them. On one occasion; feeling a cuff and sleeve pass over my hand, I said to the medium, "are you *writing* on that slate?" She said, "no; you see I have a loose sleeve on." But I insisted we should hold the slate again, — when I asked my brother to write his name, right side up to me. When we took the slate from under the table, there was my father's name, "Jesse S. Norcross," in a bold hand, right side up to me, and of course up side down to her. The question is, what science could do this except the spiritual, or an intelligent, thinking, acting individuality, whom I shall always return thanks to. I believe in God as the universal father, and the Christ as my elder brother. And why should I not believe so? for true spiritualism, teaches love to God and our fellow beings; and that there is life beyond the grave, and also that God's laws cannot be broken with impunity.

When I see so many good people suffer, and little innocent children suffer for the sins of their parents, which does not seem either generous or just; and I feel my father's spirit is so near, of him I know, and God seems a great way off. Then I ask the question, does God care for the things of earth; or having created and laid down certain laws, allows people to go through life blindfolded or in ignorance, and suffer the consequences of their ignorance, in the penalties of transgression? Sin is the transgression of God's law; and its effects extend to the third and fourth generation. Then why teach forgiveness of sin? If I forgive my child, for wrong doing, I would not cause some terrible calamity to befall them, and extend it through future generations. Theologians are to blame for presenting God to the people, in such a manner, instead of teaching men the responsibility that rests upon themselves for wrong doing; not that it is God that punishes, but we, through ignorance, do not live in harmony with his laws. Teach the world there is no forgiveness of sin, that will evade the just penalty of wrong doing; and you will rid your world of one serpent that has undermined society. And God speed the time, when the *serpent*, that, coiled at the feet of Mother Eve, will be trodden out of existence, by the heel of the women of the nineteenth century.

DESTINY.

Is there an unseen destiny,
That shapes the way of life,
And when we would be strong and true,
We find discord and strife?
And will there ever be a time,
We shall know the when and why,—
And will the veil be lifted,
If we only work and try?

If so, I would learn patience,
And certain self control;
For I would ever wish to do,
What was best for my own soul.
For I know there is a darkness,
That is darker than the night;
It's when the young and innocent,
Have felt the world's sad blight.

It's when we have lost faith in friends,
And feel that hope's all gone,
And know of human weaknesses,
And feel earth's temptations strong;
And know that all past life has been,
By circumstances ruled;
Yet, it has been to you and me,
The hardest of life's school.

And is there still a recompense,
For those who suffer, and are strong?
Or, must we go to spirit life,
A blight from other's wrongs;

I cannot feel that God, so good,
  Ordained the ways of man,
Would make a law that's so unjust,
  That we cannot understand.

Oh, no! I would rather walk by faith,
  If in blindness it need be,
Than to believe in such injustice,
  Or doubt God's immensity;
And so I live, in hope and trust,
  Though slow progression be,
Knowing that God, as with his own,
  That we must reap as we have sown.

So I will trust him to the end,
  And blow hope into life;
And will not doubt God's goodness,
  Though I see discord and strife,
Though storms may beat about me,
  And life's ship sway to and fro,
I will anchor my hopes in Heaven,
  Where ever I wish to go.

And I will trust in God that ruleth,
  The universe far and wide;
I'll cast all doubt out of my mind,
  God shall be my strength and guide;
For as I look back in the past,
  When my young feet would have strayed,
I have heard the loving voices,
  My child, be not afraid.

The cross it may be heavy,
  But bear it without a frown;
Although you may get weary,
  Its recompense a crown.

Oh! how I love the silence,
When the still, small voices, seem
To me like light in darkness,
From which my spirit gleams
It's strength and consolation,
When my body weary be,
And I am tired of earthly turmoils,
And their sad miseries.

But out of all this darkness,
Comes a Light that's bright and true;
And I hear the loving voices again,
Dear mother, we come to you.
And then there comes a holy calm,
O'er my spirit it is thrown;
And I hear the loving voices, again,
You will reap as you have sown.

Oh! my sisters, if life's reaping
Is the very seeds we've sown,
If we all must reap in spirit,
Nothing only what's our own;
Let us struggle in life's battle,
If a victory we may gain,
And renew ourselves in spirit,
Then our bounty we can claim.

And, brothers, you have all
This world upon your side;
See you deal with us so justly,
We can look to you with pride.
For you know a traitor's banner,
Can be thrown out to the breeze,
May delight you for a moment,
But can never bring you ease.

There are scenes which make us shudder,
  And with horror we despise;
If you wish to claim our homage,
  From its darkness you must rise.
You are called our earth's protectors, —
  So I bid you thus beware;
There will be a time when justice
  Will recompense, you for your care.

There is a law, called retribution,
  And it's mighty and it's just,
And you'll find God's laws are truthful,
  Obey them all we must.
There is whispering in the breezes,
  That are floating o'er our plain,
See that justice, is no longer
  Crushed, and nothing but a name.

CHAPTER XIV.

DEATH OF WILLIE.

When we carefully watch the events in human life, and the circumstances connected therewith, we cannot fail to perceive, that there seems an unseen destiny that attends us, and in some way shapes our lives, or rather that we are destined from the cradle to the grave, to do and traverse just so many winding paths, and to be hemmed in by just so many circumstances. If there was one occupation that our mother despised more than another, it was that of a mariner, or those that followed the sea. It was wholly from an ignorant prejudice concerning their mode of life, and non-association with that class of persons.

When my youngest brother (Willie) became about seventeen years old, it seemed as if a strange destiny followed him; he could get no chance to learn a trade, and everything he undertook was a failure; nothing seemed open to him, and becoming acquainted with some young men who went to sea, he felt that he must do something, and so was persuaded to go. Mother felt very badly about it; first, because she did not like the water, and then he was her youngest child. He went one voyage of a year, and returned safely; and in consequence mother's fears were lulled, and her opinion of that class of persons somewhat changed. After remaining at home a few weeks, he felt that he must leave again, but she opposed it with all her might, having an impression that something would happen to him, but to no purpose; he shipped for a voyage from Boston to San Francisco, and coming home, said to mother, laughingly, I have signed my death warrant, — meaning the shipping articles.

Oh! how many of us in jest are so truly in earnest, but the prophetic spirit within, keeps the physical, ignorant of what is to befall us. But what law is hidden, remains yet to be revealed to our outer senses. The evening before his departure, he spent at my house; I then being interested in rapping and tipping, persuaded him to sit with me at the table; when the table, which was a common card table, with the leaf turned up on to the top, and an intelligence purporting to be the spirit of my father manifested through the table, by raps and tips, told Willie not to go to California; as he had lost his life there; told him (Willie) if he went, he would never return. But Willie did not believe it, and said we were conversing with demons. He being somewhat frightened, got up and went out into the hall. The table immediately started after him; when it came to the door, the leaves closed, as it could not pass through the doorway without, it went into the hall and made as if going up the stairs. Willie begged of me to stop it, which I did; and in consequence held a conversation with him concerning the return of spirits, telling him that if he was drowned, or passed away, to come to me if possible, (this was in 1861, autumn), which he promised to do. He left home, and in due time arrived in San Francisco. There he changed vessels, and sailed for some port in Russia. The following April, as I sat sewing,—a clock on the mantle, which had no striking weight, nor had there been any on it for ten years, struck nine times. I was surprised, and did not know what to think, but did not mention it at the time, as my medium powers were troubling me, and some of my friends thought me very foolish. But on retiring that night, there came a great noise, as of persons running too and fro, the creaking of ropes, and rattling of blocks,—and, as of the hasty swinging of yards, as of men on board ship under great excitement. Then the noise went through into the next room, in which a cousin was sleeping, and I saw *my brother Willie, standing by my bed, wet, dripping with water*, and he said to me, "I was drowned last night." I arose and went into the next room, as my cousin was very much frightened, she declaring that a large lamp on the mantle shelf, had fallen, and broken in pieces on the carpet. I looked around, and found nothing disturbed The lamp was in its place, whole as before. Getting into bed with her, the bed commenced to rock like a ship at sea, giving me positive assurance it was him; since which time he has ever been with me, at intervals.

When I asked him why he could manifest to me as he did on that occasion, he said, "he died in full strength, and it was the tie that bound him to us."

Oh! the fearful knowledge, knowing your friends have passed away, and cannot prove it to others! I informed my mother that Willie was dead; she would not believe it, and begged of me not to believe such foolishness. Said it was fearful to believe such superstitions, as it would lead to or produce insanity. Oh! reader, just imagine yourself standing alone, knowing you had ample evidence of the return of father and brother, and yet those of your own family ignoring the fact, as well as strangers, and believing that you had a vivid imagination, or was laboring under a delusion. It requires courage and combativeness, in no small degree, to combat all the arguments, and all the reasons put forth, to show that such things cannot be, by the wise ones in the community.

Well, all I can say is, it has been a blessed delusion to me, that brother Willie has given me information, concerning affairs to happen, before they came upon me, that would have crushed me, had it been otherwise; and to-day I bow in humble thankfulness to God, for the intuitive perception that has blessed my life.

We did not get the news of his death till December following, when all I had told was verified by the captain of the ship in which he had sailed from San Francisco.

Being interested in temperance as well as spiritualism, I went one afternoon to hear a Mr. M., who held a meeting at Temperance Hall, in East Boston, the subject being Spiritualism. Soon after entering the hall, I came to the conclusion the lecturer had been drinking freely. I looked around, and seeing the emblems of temperance on the walls, I said, mentally, "Willie, are you here?" and immediately got a response. I said, if you are here, and feel that the lecturer is disgracing the hall, make it known to me by closing his mouth. If you do, I will address the audience myself. The lecturer arose, and after one or two attempts to speak, gave it up, and said there was some one in the hall who had an influence over him. I arose, went to the rostrum, and held the audience two hours, and there are many persons in East Boston can testify to the same.

And thus my brother has ever been watchful for my interest. If at any time he could not control me, he would go to my daughter, and tell her what he desired me to do. Some three years ago, there were clouds hanging over me and mine; and one night I was awakened from my sleep, and saw him sitting at a table, leaning his arm upon it; and he said, "Julia, do you hear the clock strike three?" and immediately the clock in the dining-room struck three. I answered, "yes." He seemed to throw an influence over my perceptive organs, and said, "you will remember this in the morning."

He then told me that I had another trouble to pass through, and related to me what it was. I sprang up in bed, and said, "I cannot bear it. You *will* prevent it." In reply, he said, "impossible; I cannot if I would; it is better now, than later in life. I can counsel you, but cannot prevent the effect of a hidden cause. So promise that you will bear it, and I will help you through; none but cowards, try to escape the responsibilities of life, and its duties. You have a maternal duty to perform; see that you are firm, and true to your womanhood. I will influence those I can to assist you; nothing shall be hidden from my eyes, and justice shall be done you and yours."

This was in May, and the trouble did not occur till the following September; when everything turned out just as he told me it would.

Great Heavens! it is not that our loved ones do not come to us, but it is our own unworthy selves, that they cannot approach, because we are so material and have so little of spiritual strength to give them to use.

Our noble boy, he is not dead,
  I cannot have it so;
He's only gone to come again,
  And help us here below.

His spirit's passed to brighter realms,
  And yet I feel him near,
Cheering me on to a nobler work,
  Yet taking away every fear.

Two months ago as we retired
  Our slumbers to obtain,
My thoughts ran wild, and off I roamed,
  And then returned again; —

Until my mind on Willie seemed
  To rest, as if a thought I gleaned;
From out the mysterious night,
  There came at once a gleam of light.

There came a tiny, little rap,
  And then were ropes a drawing back,
Then, hark; a noise so queer and strange,
  A voice from Annie's room then came,

Saying, "Julia, come; I am afraid; ope' the door;
  The lamp has fallen on the floor;"
I looked the chamber all around,
  Not a mortal thing could there be found.

I then returned unto my bed,
  Thinking and musing of the dead;
And then a quiet seemed to reign, —
  I thanked my God, and slept again.

And now I firmly do believe,
  And I myself, would not deceive,
That Willie returned to me again,
  To fulfill a promise I once obtained.

It is my faith, that makes me free
  To think of him who went to sea.
Our darling, noble, impulsive brother,
  His place is vacant, can be filled by no other.

A. D. 1862.

CHAPTER XV.

In writing the experiences of my life and its many changes, and also many strange occurrences concerning others, I expect that there will be those who will doubt the truthfulness of what I write. Be that as it may, it gives me no uneasiness, for I believe in planting the seeds of truth, and waiting God's own time to gather in the harvest.

Why, this lovely summer eve, as my pen is running over the paper, I can look back forty years, and see many things that were in darkness, have come to the recognization of light and might; and to-day, it is hardly safe to disbelieve anything, but wait for the coming light.

To-day an incident occurred in my office, which brought to mind a very singular case I had once. A Mrs. D——, of East Boston, called to see me, professionally; and while talking, asked me if I wished to know about a daughter of hers, which I miraculously cured some seven years ago; saying she was married, and weighed about one hundred and forty pounds. The girl then was (when cured) thirteen years old; she had been sick for sixteen weeks, when I was sent for to see what I thought of her. She was attended by Dr. C. and Dr. L., of East Boston. I found the girl a perfect skeleton; not having taken food for fifty-six days; nor had she opened her eyes in all that time; and the only way the mother could tell that there was life in her, was by holding a glass over her mouth, and the dampness showing that she breathed; and my surprise was that physicans could have such a case, and take so little interest in it. But poverty is often sufficient reason for wilful neglect, and lack of sympathy. But the peculiar case, and the singular circumstances surrounding it, would naturally interest a searcher after truth, or a scientist after knowledge. I am sure I learned a great lesson from that case, and have since believed in the efficacy of prayer, and truth in a higher life. The girl seemed like a snake, crawling about the bed, writhing and twisting at times, but most of the time all drawn up and motionless. My sympathy for the poor, worn out mother, and what seemed idiotic child, brought all my best feelings into action; and knowing I had been given power, at other times to relieve the sick and suffering, I felt that no disease known, could make a child appear so strange. I made an earnest prayer for her restoration to health, and gave such remedies as I thought proper; and to my utter astonishment, the words that came to my lips, seemed foreign to myself, and a feeling of power came over me. I seemed as if being lifted up; and I closed the prayer with bidding some one begone from the frail body, that lay before me. This was in the morning; in the afternoon I again visited her, and while there she opened her eyes, (which had been closed for fifty-six days,) and asked for water, which I gave her, she drinking a tumbler full. I visited her again the next morning, and while there, she asked for bread, which was given her; she ate it slowly, but not eagerly. I then ordered her a proper diet, and from that time, she improved rapidly, until she regained her health, which has been good ever since, now seven years. Experience has led me to believe that she was held by an influence outside of herself; and by earnest prayer, and my strong will, assisted by my spirit guides, she was restored to health and strength. Why believe that such things occurred in Bible times, and doubt what is happening every day in your own midst, and will not take the trouble to investigate, but pronounce false that which you can prove true with very little trouble? Mark 11: 23-24; 5: 40-43.

CHAPTER XVI.

THE STORY CONCERNING THE CURE OF MRS. B. G.

I have obtained permission of one of my patients in Yarmouth, Mass., to relate her cure; for she has outlived all the falsehoods that could be manufactured in a bigoted country town, concerning herself and family, and has risen so far above the calumnies and petty slanderers, whose chief business is to meddle with and condemn everything they cannot understand; and who think more of what they wear, than they do of what they are; and many of them are afraid of Spiritualism, because they have sins to hide,—not knowing that spirits do not come to retail slander, nor rebuke sinners, but to let the light in concerning our spiritual development for another sphere of existence; for all the higher influences see too much of unhappiness created by human beings, and see so little of that religious element that is professed, but not possessed; and while they regret the necessity of reproof sometimes, they well know that the seed of human kindness will spring up wherever sown, and all malignant slander will return unto its own. Some years ago, on one of my professional visits to East Dennis, Mass., I was called to see a lady in the town of Yarmouth. Upon entering the house, I felt sure that there was something peculiar concerning the case; although finding the lady, Mrs. G., in a very feeble condition, I seemed to feel that I should never cure her, unless she was in my own house. She was sick in many ways, but the spasms she was subject to, I was sure could not come from the physical condition, which I then found her in. She was one of those sensitive women, who have great mental strength within a weak body, and who had spirituality large, and self-esteem small; benevolence large, and withal a kind heart, which was ofttimes pierced by the unkind treatment of so-called friends, and not being well understood. Of a retiring nature, of mediumistic powers, which she knew nothing about, her religious views being strictly Orthodox Congregationalist. I saw at once she needed strength to come to my house, and I must first build her up. So I said to those who sent for me, I will give her medicine two weeks, then she must come to my house in Boston, where I will cure her of her terrible fits, or spasms. I left medicine for her, and in two weeks she was brought to my house in Boston, just two days before her husband sailed on a voyage to the East Indies. He had been at home for a number of months, waiting for a ship, he being in a business that kept him from home two years at a time. It was on his return from a long voyage that she was taken with these violent spasms and contortions, which were fearful to witness; for instance, she would become cold, and then one hand would begin to move; in a few minutes the other hand would begin to move round and round, and she would throw her head backwards and forewards; then the lower limbs drawn up till she would be doubled up into a ball; and it seemed sometimes as if every muscle in her body was contracted, and her suffering seemed intense; and for ten months these spasms had continued; and strange as it may seem, she had them worse when her husband came into the room. Of course it gave rise to gossip that he was in some way the cause of producing them. Day after day, and week after week they continued, and no physician could explain the where or the wherefore, or the cause that produced such effects. After treating her two weeks, she came to my house, arriving about seven in the evening. I had her put to bed, and asked her if she would have any thing to eat. She said, "no." I brought her a cup of tea, and sat down beside her, feeling she must be very tired, riding so far, and hoping she would not have one of her fits that night. She was very weak, and very thin of flesh; of a bilious temperament, nerves weak, and other diseases, which had been about her for years;—she not having been well for four years, keeping her bed most of the time, but had these fits in addition to her other diseases, for at least ten months. Every thing had been surmised and imagined that could possibly be thought of, in a country town; those having sympathy with her, condemning him; and those having sympathy with him, of course falsified every thing concerning her; but the day she came to my house, she seemed very much exhausted for an hour or so, when I perceived that one hand began to move, and the struggle commenced; the cords contracted in the wrists, and such a peculiar expression on the countenance. In a few minutes, the other hand commenced, and they were both drawn up, and she seemed struggling to free them. Then the head began to be drawn down to the breast, and move first one side, then the other; the limbs contracted and were drawn up, as if they were going to roll her up in a ball; and after going through these contortions for from thirty minutes to an hour, she would be completely exhausted; then relax, and go to sleep for a while, only to awake and go through the same manœuvre again. When it commenced at my house, I thought it was terrible to witness. What must it be to go through? While watching her, I placed my hand upon her head, to see if she was cold or hot, when she jumped away from me, and went against the wall, and said, with her teeth clenched together, "*No, you don't.*" I asked Mrs. G., "did you speak?" "No," she answered. I went around the other side of the bed, and placing my hand on her head again, when, "*No you don't!*" came again through the closed teeth. I was amazed. Pushing the bed back against the wall, I returned to the front side, determined to solve the mystery; and placing my hand firmly on her head, strong enough to hold her down, to my own amazement, some one placed their hand on my head so powerfully, that I was obliged to press hard against the side of the bedstead, to maintain my own equilibrium; and a feeling, I never shall forget, came over me, filling me with such a power, and I so acutely conscious of it, filling my soul with a prayer which seemed to lift me out of myself; and I listened attentively to every word as it was forced through my own lips, from the power that held me in such a strange way; and when the prayer was finished, I heard these words forced through my own lips: — "In the name of God, come out of this woman!" which was repeated three times. All struggling seemed to cease, and like one dying, she fell back, perfectly exhausted, with a sort of rattling in her throat, but I seemed myself, held by such a strange power. As she relaxed in her struggles, I lifted my hand from her forehead, and drew the clothes up over her, but could not seem to move; when looking up, I beheld a man standing at the foot of the bed, looking at me, and it seemed natural for me to say, "was that you trying to injure this woman;" when he nodded his head in answer, "yes;" when looking to see what kind of person he was, I saw that he was naked to the waist, and different from any person I had ever seen. A sort of mist arose about him, and condensed in something solid, like an iron bar, about one-half a yard long, which went right to his forehead; and immediately a stream of blood flowed freely from the wound produced. Still the strange power seemed to hold me, and he came forward and knelt at my feet. As he did so, I looked down, and there seemed something dark about him. I felt the same strange power on my brain again, with all the weight, and my hands involuntarily clasped together, and issuing from my lips came another earnest prayer; — when, behold! the dark conditions about him disappeared. He arose with a pleased look on his countenance, and went out through the corner of the room. The power being lifted from me, I turned to my patient, who was sleeping soundly, with a moist sweat on her hands and face. She slept all night, and when she awoke, I did not refer to the scene of the night previous, feeling that to tell her would frighten her; and no one else would believe such a story, and I had better wait. Giving her her breakfast and a bath, she slept most of the next day. I gave her then acute medicines, for two weeks, after which botanic medicines to restore her strength and vitality. She never had one of those fits afterwards, and in a few weeks returned to her home a well woman, to the surprise of all her friends and neighbors, and has continued so ever since, with the exception of some slight indisposition, as all are subject to.

Her husband arrived in New York, after an absence of nearly two years, and wrote to her to meet him in Boston, and they visited me whilst there. I related to him the story of his wife's cure, when to my surprise, he recognized the man from my description of him, as a "Kanaka." When he was on a former voyage to the Indies, having some Kanakas on board the ship at work, they revolted and undertook to take possession of the ship, when he, (Captain G.,) seized the first thing that came to hand, which was a marline-spike, and threw it at one of them with all his might, hitting him in the head, and killing him instantly, which had the effect to quell the mutiny and restore order.

He even went and got his mate, and brought him to hear the story from my lips, and also to verify what he had told me. After knowing both sides of this wonderful story, I asked my guides to explain to me why the innocent should suffer so much; and was told, "that the positive will to overcome is always used in such cases, and whatever weapon is used, carries with it the will of the party using it; and consequently his magnetic power, and the spirit of the injured man, returns with the rebound and attaches itself to the party injuring another." In this case the man being killed, attached himself (the spirit) to Captain G., and when he returned home, his wife being in feeble health, and consequently negative, and also being mediumistic, and wholly ignorant of the fact, the spirit left the husband and attached itself to her (the wife;) and, as in old times, it required a third and spiritual person to separate the spirits. Mark, ix.: 17—29.

My guides told me that I was left in a conscious state, that I might realize that there was a power that we could call upon to assist in the removal of evil influences, which sometimes comes in the form of disease. But we must have faith, and ask in sincerity and truth.

I have had many cases similar to this; and from what I know of spirit influence, am positive beyond a doubt, that the spirits of the departed do act more or less upon human beings; and it can be easily proved that spirits are on, or near the earth at times. Who can say that they are not here all of the time?

Will some of the more knowing ones, who tell us it is "impossible for spirits to communicate with those in the body," please to inform us if they leave the earth? For if the "body returns to dust," and the "spirit to God, who gave it," it would not have to go far, for God is everywhere. For if there is a place, where the weary are at rest, I wish to go there, for I know it would be best; where the sinner will be better, and the saints more true, where peace will reign forever. My reader, don't you?

CHAPTER XVII.

When will the time come, that will teach us to write what we know and feel to be true, is neither egotistical, nor wrong; but that every human being has not only the right, but it is their duty to do so; so much is hidden, that is actually true, — while so much is written that is false and fictitious, because it is considered as praising one's self, to give any information concerning their experiences, or what they have done for the benefit of humanity.

It has always seemed strange to me, to see men get up in a religious or temperance meeting, and tell how wicked they have been, and how much crime they have committed, and such kind of vulgarism; but you seldom hear how much good, certain persons have done. Experience has taught the world, that such men who throw themselves down upon their knees, and tell God what he already knows, what poor miserable beings they are, know themselves better than they are known. For my part, when a man is so lost to self respect, as to get up in public and tell of his degradation, I do not wish to hear it; neither do

I wish my children to, for I think the influence is bad; and it has done more to disgrace religious meetings, of a reformatory character, than any other one thing, as it keeps some of our best people from attending such meetings. Let me ask why are such things permitted?

Who would listen for one moment to a weak woman, and hear her narrate her crimes, and talk of her guilt? She would be hissed from the rostrum. Why is it less despicable, told by a man? What ruined the temperance movement, was the hypocrisy and deceit that was constantly behind the scenes. No wonder so many of the sons and daughters of Christian parents are disbelievers, when they have listened to those who have so little knowledge of the laws that control our physical being, as to boast that God has cleansed them from their sins, when every intelligent person knows that sin is the transgression of law, and observation teaches us that we cannot evade the consequences! I admit, that by an unseen law, God has permitted certain persons, with the help of an outside influence, to perform many cures, and help certain physical deformities; but the persons must be naturally sympathetic and spiritual in their make up. The reason why we have so many imitators or frauds, is not because there is no law, but because so few understand and live up to the requirements of the law.

On one of my professional visits to Yarmouth, Mass., a few years ago, I was told there was a poor man suffering with white swelling of the knee, and that the physicians, three in number, said he must have his leg taken off. When I heard it, my sympathies were aroused for the sufferer; not only was the man suffering from disease, but he had not the wherewith to help himself, being exceedingly poor. I went to see him,* and this is what transpired.

I became entranced, and made a prayer, which he said thrilled him through and through; and while in that state, told him he should be well in a few days, and his limb as good as the other. They who controlled me, proved their power, by helping him; and showed to the world what a power could come through a weak woman. I bathed the limb, and ordered a vinegar poultice applied. His sufferings were intense for a few hours from the effect of the influence thrown upon him, when the pain began to cease, the swelling to subside, and in four days the limb was well as the other, and has remained so. He is eighty-four years old, and last summer walked three miles to camp-meeting, and back again the same day. I had not seen him in all that time, four years, since I made the night visit.

I believe that those who try to do their duty and the will of God, (not through fear, but by faith,) by

---

* Gorham Taylor, Yarmouth, Mass.

assisting those who cannot help themselves, and are weak and suffering, are acted upon through their sympathetic natures, by the spirit influences delegated for that purpose.

The messengers God sends to assist us and strengthen human hearts, to alleviate human suffering, do not come to make money, but come because of the sympathy that the child of earth has for humanity, and they leave the money question entirely to the honesty of the person and their good judgment. It is absurd to hear people undertake to tell who shall judge of my financial affairs, who I shall charge, and who treat free? 2, Kings, Chap. 5. My guides assist me because I try to be worthy of their love and confidence; and my organization is adapted to their use. I am grateful for their assistance and help, but they never undertake to manage my earthly affairs.

This accounts for the failure of many mediums; they sit down, and expect the spirits will paddle them into safe water. But there are spirits I would not trust out of the body, any more than I would trust them while in it. For the world has too long tampered with sin, to expect to do away with it in any other way than by the elevation and education of the people. It has too long allowed might to trample upon right, because right is apt to be non-resistant, forgetting that God is all strength, and uses the weak things of the earth to overcome the strong; and it is evident to all thinking minds, that God makes use of earth's children and their organization, to advance the natural and spiritual sciences, as fast as the human race can bear it. We all observe that no great discovery is ever made by human beings, until the world has need of it, and we are ready to accept it; and we also see that there are those who always oppose every advance movement, and will always cry fraud, until opposition ceases to be the popular side; when they will quietly say they always believed so-and-so. But thanks to a beneficent God, opposition is the twin sister to progression, and brings out the dormant faculties of our natures, for I believe there are very few persons, but that can give us something in regard to this question of the day,—Spirtualism, or the law of communication with the unseen intelligences.

I was once acquainted with a man, who was, or appeared to be a sincere Methodist, a great worker in the church, and I believe he felt that he was honest in his work. But it did not satisfy his soul; for, according to his belief, God *afflicted* him more than he was able to bear; as one child sickened and died, then another; and finally, the last, and only one, was burned to death, which made his wife sick at heart. She was also very active in church affairs; at last she became in such a state of mind, that she wished to retire from the world, believing that God was afflicting her for some unknown sin. And in consequence she went away amongst the Shakers.

Oh! what a consolation would a belief in spirit communion have been to that broken-hearted mother! how it would have strengthened in her God's love and goodness, and taught her that her loved ones were waiting for her in the summer land. It is no wonder that he became reckless and doubting. It is no wonder, with such a belief, that he ignored everything pertaining to religion. He even doubted the honesty of the Shakers, and determined not to go there, after his wife had made her mind up to stay the rest of her life. He is not the only human soul that has been shipwrecked by false theology. Time wore on, the wife amongst the Shakers; he went recklessly about the world, left the little town of M., and after a time, married again, this time an Orthodox Congregationalist, and became again converted, and joined the church. What hypocrisy! He did not dare to act himself,—tortured by conscience, that never sleeps, and trying to swallow that which has been taught by another creed, equally as false, nothing but simple faith to cling to, no positive evidence. In this frame of mind he sought me, hearing that I had said I not only believed, but had positive knowledge of spirit communion. He said he was worse off than before, and only asked that he might be led aright. I told him to pray to God, to give him the light, not through the church, but to his own spirit. I did not see him again for years, and that just before he died.

He sent for me, to tell me he had seen the Light, and would die in a few weeks: telling me that he wanted me to tell this story to every man or woman who was in spiritual darkness: and I put it in this book, to cheer some doubting one, to read after I am gone, to meet my loved ones in the spirit home.

This is his story: — "I arose one morning about four o'clock, to go out to attend to my business, and finding it too early, took the cushion off a chair and laid down by the stove; and as soon as I had laid down, some one took me by the arm, and said, 'come with me;' we went out at the front door into the yard; then the spirit said to me, 'we must get into the wind, so as to be lifted to the air above.' Soon we were lifted off our feet and could see everything below. We floated in the air till we reached Boston, (Salem, Mass., being his place of residence,) where we visited the hospitals, and saw the physicians dissect human bodies; after which we went to New York, visiting the various hospitals; the guide said it was that I might see how much suffering there was. Visited also other countries, which I was told was to instruct me concerning human life. He told me to remember all I saw; and he also touched my perceptive organs, that I might remember. He told me that he, the guide, would give me a glimpse of the spirit world; as all knowledge is from that world, transmitted through human organizations. He showed me a beautiful, open plain, laid out in paths as far as the eye could see, looking like a massive grass plot, on which were numerous little white tents. I turned to my guide, and asked what it meant. He answered, 'in my father's house are many mansions; if it were not so I would have told you.' Then he led me from one to another of these tents. I noticed that some were occupied and some were not. I asked the reason of it. He told me that some were living on the earth yet. As we passed along, I noticed that some of the tent doors were closed, and the names were on the doors; on one of which I read, H. P. C., my own name, aged fifty-seven years. I asked the reason of this, and was told that in eight weeks I should occupy that tent. My guide now said, we must return to earth. I begged him to let me remain, but he said I must return and relate what I had seen, that he would come for me again; as we came towards earth, I met many persons which I knew. They would salute to us and pass on. All seemed to be travelling in the air, the same as we were; some of them would have a guide hold of them, but most of them were travelling without. I asked what it meant, and was told, those to whom the guide is connected must return to earth to inhabit the physical body for a while; those without, have died and are separated from the body. As we came near home, we met a lady who was one of my near neighbors; as I spoke to her, I told my guide that she lived very near me, with her sister. 'Well,' said he, 'she is dead and buried, since you came away.' As we came near my house, we met the other sister. I told him, (the guide) that was the other sister. He said, 'she is dead, but will not leave the earth till her body is buried. I then came to my own house, where I found my body stretched on a bed which the guide said, I must enter again, for a while. As soon as I came to myself, I asked my wife concerning the neighbors. She evaded my question, till I told her I had seen them both in the spirit world, and knew they were dead. When she told me that they had both died with diptheria, whilst I lay unconscious, I wanted to tell my wife what I had seen, and that I believed I should die in eight weeks; but she would not listen to me, and said it was all a dream, or the vagaries of a disordered brain. So I sent for you, Mrs. C., as the doctors say it was apoplexy which I had." He recovered so as to be able to go out, went to an insurance office, got his life insured for three thousand dollars, for the benefit of his wife and child, and in eight weeks had a second attack and died. I went to his funeral in Salem, Mass.

CHAPTER XVIII.

At one time I stepped into a clairvoyant's office, to inquire for some one, and found the lady engaged; and while waiting in the reception room, a gentleman, in advanced years, well dressed, and intelligent appearing, came in, and after waiting awhile — asked me if this lady, the one who kept the office, was a clairvoyant. "I think she is," was my reply. "Well, I don't believe anything at all, in clairvoyance," said he. I said to him, "did you ever stop to think that it never changed a *fact*, because you did not believe in it? I will give you a test of clairvoyance, and it shall not cost you anything. Standing by your side is a young man, who committed suicide, and wants to see his mother very much, as she is nearly broken-hearted on account of it; and you do not know why he did so. His name is Charley." I then arose to go out, when he said, "why! don't leave me so. Where do you live?" I handed him my card. He inquired how soon I could go to see his family. This was on Monday; I visited them on the following Thursday,and while there, personated the young man, by putting a handkerchief about my neck, in the same way that his was when found. I then gave his message to his father, mother and sisters. He passed away three years before. I had never met any of the family or ever heard of them, and they were entirely ignorant of spirit communion. Was that not sufficient evidence of the return of the spirit of the departed to them? It was; and I know that if Dr. S., of Reading, was asked the question, he would not deny the fact. So, reader, doubt nothing, but strive to understand all things, and thank God that all knowledge was not given to the great and learned; but God takes the weak to confound the strong.

Some four years ago I was in Saxonville, on business connected with my profession, and while there, stopping at the house of Mr. A., I had wonderful manifestations, by raps, as soon as I retired at night; so much so, that I spoke to the family about it. Any one in the hall could hear the raps, as I was talking with them. I was intending to remain until Saturday, but on Tuesday was told by my spirit friends, to go home at once, as there was a letter on my office table, with bad news in it. I went the same afternoon, and found the letter on my table. My spirit friends, E. C. and Willie, were there, and it makes me tremble, and the tears will fall, when I think how I suffered in reading that letter, and how kind my spirit friends were in advising me what to do,—brother Willie telling me just who to go to for advice and assistance, they (the spirits) telling me it was their time to help me, as I had helped them. E. C. was a young woman, who thought her life had been shortened by her surroundings, and whose mother was a dear friend of mine. I shall always remember her kind sympathy in connection with my spirit brother, and the advice they gave me in my trouble, when earthly friends seemed to stand aloof, fearing they might intrude. Then did I realize, more than ever, the power of the unseen, whose strength seemed to increase when we need their aid. This same young lady came to me once, and told me her husband's mother had a cancer; begged of me to go and see her, and do all I could for her; not that they harmonized on the earth, but to give her spirit light, that she (the mother) might not continue in spiritual darkness; and also that she (the spirit E. C.) might see her husband and child. I have many times at her request, left my office and gone into that house, that she might see her child. I believe, in fact I know, that the spirits use a medium's brain and eyes to see and know what is taking place in the physical world.

The spirit of this same young woman, has many times been to me in my office, and taken messages from me to her mother, at the seashore, where she would attract her mother's attention by raps, and then communicate with her, and tell her what I had said.

She has asked me to go to her father's house, when they are in the city, that she might converse with them. After manifesting in various ways and through different mediums, and convincing her friends beyond a doubt, of her existence in spirit, she seemed to have accomplished her work. She then told me if I wished for her, to call for her, and she would come. She said, "there were those on earth she loved, but could not approach, they were so wrapped up in material things." I asked her if it did not make her feel sad. She answered, "they have an eternity to outlive it in."

I was called to visit a patient who had been attended by Dr. I., of East Boston, when, after returning to my office, I found that I had company. A tall gentleman, a spirit with full sandy beard, light hair, and blue eyes, seemed to be close to me, walking by my side. I asked him what he wanted. In reply, he said, "I want to see my brother Richard." I asked who he (the spirit) was; he said his name was "P. Ingalls."

I immediately wrote a note to his brother, asking him to call at my office at his earliest convenience. When he came I said to him, a spirit brother of yours has come to me, and I do not wish to be annoyed by any one's friends; and the only way to prevent it, is to let him give his communication. You may laugh or say what you please; to me it is a sacred duty, as

I feel there is a responsibility resting upon me. Then he said, "let us know what it is." The spirit said to him, "Richard, the redeeming trait in your character is love for me;" which seemed to affect the Doctor very much. He then said, "arrange your worldly affairs in a proper manner, so that there would be no trouble if any one else had the settlement of them. My health broke down by the transgression of natural laws. I am permitted to warn you. You have habits that must be overcome, or you'll come to me before the snow falls in November." (This being in the early spring.)

The rest of the conversation was of a private nature. Suffice it to say, he was taken sick the last of October, and died in November, before snow fell.

I told a number of my friends of the prediction, that they might watch coming events; and he, Dr. I., told his friends, but did not give them the name of the medium; and after he died there was great inquiry for the lady who had predicted his death so long before.

CHAPTER XIX.

MRS. H. E. A., DEVELOPED.

At the age of twenty-three years, my daughter, Mrs. H. E. Allen, surprised me by having her mediumistic gifts developed, I not realizing she had them; and knowing how much mediums suffer, had never encouraged it in her, and she had never manifested any desire or interest in it whatever. I should naturally have opposed it, knowing the suffering and opposition sure to follow, from a lack of appreciation by relatives and friends. Matt., x.: 34—38.

When her youngest child was about a week old, Mrs. W., the nurse, came to me, and called me to Mrs. A.'s room to see what was the matter, as it was so cold all of a sudden. It seemed as if a large wheel was in motion in the room. I went, and was surprised, as I had never seen anything like it before. Mrs. Allen seemed to be sleeping, and yet it was so cold you could not lay on the bed beside her. We placed quilts at the windows, but it done no good. The stove, with a hot fire in it, had no effect. The air seemed to be in motion, and after a time she seemed to be talking to some one. Then it became quiet, and the motion ceased. In a few days she complained of seeing faces on the window curtain, and persons moving about her. She not being well, I felt very much annoyed, as I had never seen any such manifestations before, and did not wish it. But the influence would not depart, and after a few weeks I had no power to control her, neither had she any power to control it. But they would come and talk with her, and she seemed to be in communion with an intelligence different from any thing I had ever seen. It continued thus till the morning of June fourth, when she came down from her room partly dressed, semi-conscious, and addressed me as Madame, and asked if the next day would not be her birth-day; and requested me to dedicate her to them, by decorating my room with flowers, and inviting our friends to witness her coming out as a Musical and Inspirational Medium, telling me they had been about her for many years, and were going to educate her. She being a natural musician, and I not having the means, they would act as her teachers, and any one who has heard her play, will see they have done all, and more than was promised. The names of her musical control, were, Ralph, a German, Bianski, an Italian, and Helena, an American lady. She has many others, but these are the leading ones. At this time, a gentleman connected with the press was invited in to see her, and wrote the following:

"Mrs. H. E. Allen, who resides in East Boston, has been in process of development several months. At times her inner sight was opened, and she became conscious of mingling with beings of a higher order than those of earth, amid scenes of dazzling beauty, and then of hearing seraphic music, and the eloquence of immortality, 'in thoughts that breathe and words that burn.' The stream of life, like the vision of Mirza, swept before her in endless procession, with its hopes and fears, to be followed by the dull monotony of earth. Scenes like these were often presented to her, but she did not understand their import. Of a common-sense turn of mind, she asked the utility of them. From childhood, she had been a believer in the immortality of the soul, and the truths of the sacred Scriptures. Her mother, Mrs. Julia A. Crafts, possessed mediumistic power of high order; so there did not seem any need of extra evidence to convince her of spiritual intercourse, and she certainly had no desire to become a public medium. While turning these thoughts over in her mind, she heard a voice say, 'wait and see. You will receive a birth-day present, and the future will unfold your powers.' More was said, but this embraced its substance. The night preceding the anniversary of her twenty-third birth-day, was the most interesting of her whole life.

Though conscious of laying in bed, she was taken in spirit to a splendid mansion, and found herself the center of a brilliant assembly of all ages and sexes, every one of whom knew her intimately, and congratulated her on the happy occasion. There was shaking of hands, music and dancing, and all the innocent delights of earth spiritualized, and the scene was kept up most of the night. Towards morning the company separated, wishing her many returns of the anniversary, and she sank into a sound sleep the moment the last visitor disappeared. The next day her inner sight was permanently opened, and this was the gift promised her. Several young friends who had passed out of the form, came to her personally, and requested that those near to them should be sent for, as they desired to communicate with them. In several cases, the tests of the communications received were beyond question. She differs from most mediums in this, that she sees each spirit who writes through her, and if the writing is not coherent, she immediately pauses and asks the spirit what is meant, so there may be no mistakes. She has the assurance that in the course of a few months, the spirits will be able, in her presence, to speak face to face with those who are in sympathy with them. The fact that she sees the spirit who writes through and by her, and can communicate with it, is a gift possessed by so few, that it may be considered a new phase of mediumship.

All that was promised, and even more, has been verified through Mrs. A."

In about a year after her first control, she became very ill. Indeed her life was despaired of. She would not have any physician but her mother, not realizing how hard it was to be mother and physician. After three weeks sickness, I determined to have a lady physician to consult with me; did not tell Mrs. A. about it. When the lady came she went into Mrs. A.'s room, looked at her, felt her pulse, came out into the dining-room, and said to me, "your daughter will not live till morning." It shocked me. I stepped into her room; as I did so, she lifted her hand, and made motion as if to write. I got paper and pencil. She wrote, "send that woman from the house; Hattie is not going to die." Signed, "Willie."

Soon a control influenced her who called himself "Dr. Fitz," and through her own lips, told me that she would not die, "but to give her a cup of tea and some wine crackers, so that he might vomit her." Then he raised her upon her feet, and threw her heavily upon the bed, where she lay quiet for some time; the hemorrhage ceased and she began to recover, and soon regained her usual health.

She has had three very severe fits of sickness, and every time the same influence, Dr. Fitz, has come, and through her own lips, told me what to do. At one time she lay unconscious for hours, with every muscle rigid, — when he wrote on her hand, "Give Tincture of Lobelia," which relieved her at once. At another time he ordered her "put into a carriage and ride five miles," which was done, and she recovered. For the same disease, earth physicians would not allow them to be moved in bed; which disease is considered incurable by the regular physicians.

When these spirit physicians have come to us in our need, we place the fullest confidence in them; and experience has taught us that they never fail those who trust them. I write this, simply with regard to myself and daughter, not knowing the experience of others.

Mrs. A. sailed in a steamer for Sydney, C. B., with her children, and every night my brother Willie came and informed me just how they got along while on the water; and when she arrived, she wrote me, that "Uncle William made quite a sailor of her, making her get up early, and go on deck, telling her it would prevent her being sea-sick."

It is now eight years, and her guides have been very faithful to her, teaching her to play the piano, and assisting her in many ways, and as she is naturally spiritual, she draws that kind of influence about her. But, my reader, let me impress upon your mind that there is much suffering attending a mediumistic life; your susceptibility to surrounding influences, and keenness of perception, and sensitiveness, which is a source of great annoyance, and sometimes physical suffering; — for, like a telegraph operator, the spirits of your departed friends or acquaintances, come to us to send their messages, and we don't feel like going to their friends, so will ofttimes suffer, as their friends might be opposed to such a belief.

Sometimes persons will come to Mrs. A., and influence her, so that it will make her sick, by throwing their disease upon her, which they passed away with, when she will come to me, and I will reason with them, and tell them how they injure her, and explain to them just as if they were present in the body, when they will be satisfied. Yet there are persistent ones, that will not yield, but are determined to reach their friends. Bear in mind, reader, that true mediums are not mediums from choice, but it comes to them, and they are obliged to accept it. Sometimes a high and sensitive control offers themselves to a medium; if not accepted, will go away and make room for others.

When Mrs. A. first became controlled, she would take a pencil, and write page after page of hieroglyphics and symbols. We could not read it, nor find any one that could, and being opposed by her husband, he fearing it might hurt her, she gave it up, and that class of influences would not stay, unless wanted, while another class would be more persistent and remain.

Mrs. A's influences are peculiar. When playing the piano, the influence comes on the sensorium, passing down through the arms and hands, touching the keys lightly but firmly. Musicians say it cannot be utilized, as the touch cannot be learned, but is peculiar to herself. She is conscious, but does not care to converse, unless some spirit tells her their friends are in the room, then she will give the message quite readily.

CHAPTER XX.

Then the blessed gift of seeing. One of my first experiences was in church. One Sunday morning, being interested in the sermon, when I noticed I could not see the minister, for a mist that came up before my eyes; and a man with a surplice on, stood before me, and held towards me the Bible, open, and it was right side up to me, and wrong side up to him. I read the chapter through. It was the twelfth chapter of first Corinthians. When I looked up in his face to see what it meant, he said, "*Read, Reflect;*" and dissolved with the mist.

At another time, I saw a lady sitting back to me, in a mist, same as before, and her hair from her head fell all about her. I was waiting and watching intently to see her turn her head, that I might see who it was, when a face came close to mine, and a voice said, "*many as the hairs of thy head, shall thy blessings be, if thou wilt take up the cross and follow me.*"

At another time, I saw a child laying upon a pillow as if sleeping, and I noticed how peculiarly it lay on the pillow. Six weeks afterwards I was called hastily to see an infant which was only three weeks old, that choked to death by the breaking of a blood vessel in its head, and I staid to lay it out. After placing it on a pillow, and laying it on a settee, I went to see if its head was right; when to my astonishment, there was the same child handed to me on a pillow, in church, three weeks before it was born.

I ask the question, do others learn their lessons in the same way, or have any such experiences? I explain it in this way. My guides wish to make me self-reliant, and by showing me these things it made me interested, and they chose the time when I was most negative; and that would naturally be, when my mind would be listening to another preaching. Another beautiful way our friends have of manifesting to us, is by touch. I will be reading, when some one will touch me. I always speak aloud to them, and thank them, to let them know I feel their presence: and they will stand beside me, and talk to me, and will sometimes tell me of some one that is coming to see me; and many other strange things. Sometimes I know at once who it is; at other times I cannot tell who it is. It does not seem strange to me, as they have come in the same way for so many years. Do we not often speak of our friends in the body, and have them come in very soon, showing that we feel the influence of their mental telegraph? for when we think of persons or places, we go there in thought.

So when the persons thought they would call on us, their spirit in thought preceded their body, and we caught it at once, This has been verified in three cases in our office to-day.

A few weeks ago, Mrs. A. was on the street, going to the city to call upon her mother, when a voice said to her, "your mother will be at your house in a few minutes;" when she turned about and went home, meeting her mother at the door just going in.

When Mrs. A. was first controlled, she could see some one in spirit form beating time for her as she played the piano; sometimes a lady, at others a gentleman, and after a time they would exercise her hands, and play very rapidly; at other times would play nothing but octaves, and so on, till she became proficient as a player; they never allow her to use notes, and many pieces which she plays, she has never heard; yet they prove to be the composition of some of the great masters.

At one time I went to East Dennis, Mass., which is just off the line of railroad, about four miles from the station. It happened that I was the only passenger in the mail carriage from the depot. Arrived about noon, and stopped at Mr. J. H.'s. The carriage left me at the house, went to the post office, (a little store near by) and left the mail, returned, and in going to the stable in the rear of the house passed the dining-room windows. We had just got seated at the table for dinner; as the carriage passed, I saw a man get out and come up on the piazza, as if to come in at the door; when instead he came right up to the window and disappeared; in a moment I felt a touch on my head, and a voice said: "Say to those present (there were ten of us at the table) that John Picket dropped dead in a concert room, in Philadelphia, night before last, and a notice of my death is in the mail bag." I immediately told them. They were very much surprised, and a lady present said, it was her daughter's husband's father, but that he was well a few days before. The post-master sat at the table, and heard what was said, went out and brought in the letter to Mrs. S. H., which verified the truth of the spirit's presence and statement; it also told many other things quite as strange. Mrs. H. left that afternoon for Philadelphia, to attend the funeral, where she remained with her daughter. Some two years after Mrs. S. H. sickened and died, and was brought to East Dennis for burial by her son-in-law, and after the funeral, he having been told about his father coming to me, he came to Boston to see me, and wanted a sitting. I did not know him, never having seen him before, and told him that I gave no sittings to any one only for medical examinations, but there were test mediums who made a business of it. He insisted, saying he had very singular reasons for wishing it. I said, drawing a little table up to me, put your hand on this table, and we will see if I can tell you anything, but I never go into a trance for this kind of business for any one. I had no sooner laid my hands on the table than I saw a coffin with the word "Rest," "S. H." on the plate, a life insurance policy unsigned, a lady with an infant in her arms, and a sister with her. "You must be a great medium," I said, "as I am in my normal condition, and see very strange things." I heard a voice say, "Tell him John Picket is here. He is my son." The gentleman said he had come on purpose, as Mrs. S. H. had requested him to, when he came on with her body, and the persons I saw were all deceased members of his family. It was the means of changing his religious views, and he is now the leader of a spiritual society in Shreeveport, La.

A few weeks ago a friend of mine died very suddenly; about ten days before her death, she called upon me, and I told her I had been very anxious about her, and was impressed that she must take care of herself. You know you can have some of your flesh taken off, for I fear apoplexy. I then said I have wanted to see you, as your daughter, Mrs. E. C., has influenced me concerning you, and at last I told her to send you here. After chatting awhile in a friendly way, I said, "Well, you and I know spirit communion to be a reality; and if you pass away, I know it would be the most natural thing in the world for you to come to me, or for me to come to you." And when she left that day, my impression was so strong, I should never see her again alive, that I could not contain myself, but flung myself into a chair, and began to cry. My husband coming in, was alarmed, thinking I had heard bad news; but when told what it was said: "You are very foolish; you cannot alter anything. Why feel so miserable." I said, "Because some one is telling me thus and so." But I drove it from my mind. Who will tell me where those sad forebodings come from, or why the shadows fell over me, if there is not something to impress our spirits. Shortly after she fell in the street, was taken into a house, and lay in an unconscious state three days, and passed over.

While we were expecting her death I became convinced that I should know when she passed away, although at a distance from her, and hearing in the morning she could not live an hour, expected she had passed on, but still thought I should know. At twenty minutes past eight o'clock in the evening, I felt some one grasp my arm, and call me by name; my husband being present, we looked at the clock and made a note of it. When he went to inquire at what time she died, was told she passed away at seven o'clock and forty minutes, (or twenty minutes to eight). This was on Monday evening; the next Friday, about half-past five, she came and manifested by raps, and I talked with her for more than an hour; giving us further evidence of communication with loved ones. It would be no satisfaction for us to deceive ourselves, and some persons talk as if we did not prove anything. Why, we are the most severe in our investigations, and believe nothing unless given in the most reliable way. Sceptics and unbelievers have no idea of the ways and means we use to prove whether it is our friends or not; we do not believe all we hear or see, but "prove all things and hold fast to that which is good." I have no more doubt that Mrs. L—— came to me than I have that the sun rose this morning.

Open the door, God's angel of peace;
Give all the children of earth their release:
Give man the knowledge that selfishness and sin,
The bigoted priests, have striven to keep in.
Tell all God's children to believe, never doubt,
As the kingdom of God is within, not without.

CHAPTER XXI.

A young man, a member of the Boston fire department, was killed at a fire in the city. We were neither of us, (myself or daughter,) acquainted with him or his friends; but he had heard of me as a medium, and made light of it before his death, never thinking it would be an avenue which he would avail himself of after he had been emancipated from the physical body; and while his body was being carried to Mt. Auburn, he came to my guides, and wished me to write to his mother, as soon as she returned from the funeral, as it would in a measure restore her to herself, he being "afraid she would lose her mind." None of my controls or guides could give his ideas. Only the poet could give his feelings expression, through me, he had so recently and suddenly passed away. This is what they improvised for him, on that occasion, and I sent it to his mother.

"Just over there, from the din and the darkness,
When all the shadows have passed away,—
Just over there, I was met with such gladness,
Out from earth's tabernacle I hardly could say.

Just over there, with its joy and glory,
When my dark vision was first cleared away,
Just over there, can I tell all my story,—
Thought I, what father and mother would say.

Oh, my dear father, when memory gathered,
All the past incidents came to mv view;
Oh, how in anguish, I first did discover,
I, for a while, must be parted from you.

Then, Oh, dear mother, how memory lingered
Around the dear words I last heard from you;
Then came the thought, that God, in His goodness,
Had shown me a way; I could bid you adieu.

Just over there, with all suffering ended,
Thought I of bright hours, hardly pass'd away,
And the sweet voice, as with mine it blended,
With music and laughter, as happy as day.

Just over there, from sister and brother,
Came I to consciousness, standing alone;
When the great law of attraction made pathway,
And by your sorrows, I was attracted to home.

Oh! such a scene as met my returning,
From the sad hearts and anguish of home;
And I so struggled, like a man that was drowning,
To say I am here! loved ones, do not mourn.

I know the place vacant, and the form that is absent,
Can never be filled by another but me;
But I come, tho' unseen, by your mortal vision,
So hear my soft whispers, I'm coming to thee.'

Oh! father, and mother, and sister, and brother,
And her whom I loved, when my body was free,
Just over there where my spirit is waiting,
I am watching and waiting my loved ones for thee.

Tell all my comrades, who fought the great battle
With me, side by side, in the duties of life,
If true to our souls, no matter if rattle
Brick walls, and rubbish, and fire in the strife.

Tell all our friends, who in sympathy mourn me,
All their kind thoughts arise but to bless;
And after I'm stronger, if God's laws are willing,
I'll do all I can for their happiness.

So mother, dear mother, my thoughts still linger
Around thy loved image; they always will be,
For God, in His wisdom, has done well by His children,
And by His great love I'm returning to thee.

Oh! father, be strong; don't bow down in sorrow,
But look to the realm where I'm waiting for thee;
And think how much better, to fall in life's duties,
Than by earth's temptations, as many you see.

I heard the sweet music, and saw the commotion
Within our church, so much loved by thee,
And heard my loved pastor, in words that so kindly
In sympathy to you, and so loving to me.

And when all your toils and duties are ended,
And I am then joined to some spirit band,
I'll come with such music as we have in heaven,
And bear all my loved ones, to our bright summer land.

One summer evening, not long since, I was tired and thought I would retire early. At about eight o'clock commenced to make preparations, when a hand touched me, and some one said, "go at once to 29 Buckingham St., you are wanted." I was surprised, as I was then living in East Boston, (132 Princeton St.,) and it would at least take an hour to go from where I lived, provided I caught a car on time. My brother, O. W. N., had a room at 29 Buckingham St., which he occupied when in the city; a nephew kept the house. I put my things on, took my medicine bag and started, and entered the house just after the bell struck nine, looked into the room where my niece sat sewing, and asked, "is O. W. in?" "No," said she, "I've not seen him to-day." I said, "I was over here, and have something to leave in his room." Nothing daunted by her saying he was not in, I went up to the room, and it was dark; opened the door, when some one said, "who's there?" I said, "it's I;" and there was my brother; he had come to his room sick; knowing my niece was a feeble woman, he did not let her know; and I assure you, he was very glad to see me, and my medicine satchel. I stayed and cared for him, and while there, had many pats on my shoulders, as if they (the spirits) were pleased because I had paid attention to them, in coming to help my brother. I gave the credit to my darling spirit brother, William.

Every one will remember the winter of 1857-58; — how much suffering there was and how many there were that had to have assistance, that never before or since have needed aid from the public charities. I was serving on a committee to distribute money to that class. One morning, while sitting in my room sewing, some one (in spirit) came hurriedly to my side, and whispered in my ear, go and see Mrs. H., giving street and number, — saying they have shut off the water from her house this morning, and she has neither wood nor coal. I could not believe it, as she was a widow, with two sons. I thought she would feel insulted, so I told the spirit how I felt about it, as she owned the house. They answered, "she cannot eat the house, and they won't trust her for water." So I went and told her that some one had been talking to me. She seemed much surprised, and burst into tears, and said one of her sons was sick, and the other was out of work. I had never known her husband in life, and had not seen her for months. That spirit, whoever it was, must have known that I was on that committee, and had money to assist her. Who could have given me that information, if it was not some spirit friend interested in her welfare?

That very same winter I was sick with congestion of the lungs, and one night I coughed so, that I was obliged to take medicine every half hour. I set my lamp so that I could see the clock during the night. At about twelve o'clock, I heard whispering about my bed. I sat up to see what it was, when a woman, tall and thin, with her hair combed straight back, with a plain black dress on, hooked up in front, stood before me; I thought it a warning of my death at first, but she glided past me, looking me steadily in the face, and said, "save N., save N." I had a friend many miles away by that name, and seemed to realize at once that he was in danger. I also knew that his mother died before I was born. While wondering what all this could mean, a sleepy sensation came over me, and the next I knew, I was walking the streets of Cincinnati, looking up at the houses, as if reading the numbers; when I came to No. — on a certain street, I went into the house, and there sat N., chatting with another person. I could hear their conversation, and remember how smokey the atmosphere seemed to be; yet I never was in Cincinnati in my life. Next morning I wrote to him, telling him I had had a strange vision, and asked him what he was doing that his mother could not rest, and wanted me to save him from. To my astonishment, in less than a week he came to Boston to see me about it, and that saved his life; as we afterwards learned that a plot had been laid to take his life, and get him out of the way, on account of jealousy.

CHAPTER XXII.

Alice Dean, a lovely spirit, who came to me the first year after I became controlled, (eighteen years ago,) told us that she had died of disappointment, or a broken heart. Though young in years, she had no desire to remain on earth; but after resting in spirit life eight years, she came to me, that through me she might finish, or continue her work. After prayer, by Dr. Kittredge, my control, she would influence me and sing. She was very lovely in disposition, and enjoyed visiting my patients with me, and encouraging them; it would quiet them, and give them a great deal of happiness. When she first came to me, she approached me spiritually; as I did not repulse her, she felt that she could help me, and in many of the long years I have passed through, amidst the cares and troubles of life, she has improved her own condition by helping me bear my burdens, and thrilling my soul with song, and throwing over me her love and sympathy, assuring me that she gave way physically, because of her allowing disappointment and deception to prey upon her mental, and to use up all the vital forces of the body, and in consequence passed from earth. How many women of to-day, sink under mental burdens, preferring to die young, rather than to put forth the energy to overcome the obstacles that surround, and the evils that beset them, when they should persevere to the end, working themselves out of their condition, by feeling that the duties of life are essential to their own growth, both mental, and spiritual. Oh, woman, although men may call us the weaker vessels, it is not always the stronger vessel that out-rides the storm.

So if we do not get that encouragement, which is our due, from mankind, let it teach us that God's design is, that we have more intuition than man, and in consequence are stronger in those finer powers; and so what has been denied us in physical strength, is given more abundantly in intuitional perception. Be thankful it is so, as what the mother sees, thinks, and reads, developes the brain of her children. And I know my sisters would be more careful what is around and about them, and would try to cultivate more of those powers that tend to elevate the human race, did they know that it is the prenatal condition that blesses or curses their children. Would they continue in this listless state did they realize that what the mother's read, saw, or acted, or whatever affects the conditions that surround the mother, is indelibly stamped upon her offspring? Genesis xxx: 32—43.

Look around and about us to-day, and see the blasted men and women, those that have been cursed before they saw the light; and if you heard them as I do, you too would realize, that they are not ignorant of what has befallen them; they know too well that man's dissipations, and woman's lack of firmness, is filling the world with sorrow, suffering and infidelity. For when we find the children of Christian parents, with the mark of Cain stamped upon them, we well know that nothing can be hidden from the eye of nature's God; and so children of Christian parents act out in their lives, conditions that were thrown about them in secret; and those fathers and mothers know the why and wherefore, and go on believing that God afflicts them for their good, when it is their own transgression of God's law, that is stamped upon their children; "there are none so blind as those that have no wish to see."

But I return thanks to thee, oh, loving spirit sister, who came to my spirit, when my body was tired out, and with that blending of soul sympathy, has given me such encouragement, that has strengthened my hand, upheld my spirit, and made my weary feet walk over all the obstacles in my pathway.

Let others doubt spirit communion. They too, may drink life's bitter cup, and when they do, they too, will lose faith in the selfish love and false sympathy, that comes from the human race, and like me, will hold up their hands toward the unseen realm, and feel the clasp of loving hands, and truly sympathetic souls, and hear the loving voices whisper, *it will not always last;* be true, be brave, and all will be well.

Oh, my soul, what means this sadness?
Wherefore, and why art thou cast down?
Let thy spirit go forth in gladness, —
Here's the cross, and there's the crown.

If thou art weary of life's conflicts,
And thy soul is nearly drowned,
Come what may, be always ready
To bear the cross, and wear a crown.

If in moments of temptation
Look thou up, but never down;
Bow in reverence to life's duties,
Bear the cross, you'll wear a crown.

Here's our mediums, heaven bless them;
Sickness and sorrow may on them frown;
They have seen their hours of sadness,
Bore the cross, now wear a crown.

No doubt the crosses of life, are in time, if we strive to do right, all worked out for our good, and the discipline we receive oftentimes strengthens us, and makes us firm in resisting the many temptations of life; and we should all consider, that what may look right to us, understanding all sides of our own life, may look very differently to those who only see us from their standpoint; they might be charitable to us, if they could see us in the light we see ourselves, but we should hold our own individual rights so sacred, that their blessings, or curses, can have no effect whatsoever upon us; for the saints are so few, and the sinners so many, and God so good, and man so prone to evil, that we should exercise our own sovereignty, or will, and strive for the right, regardless of what the world may say or do. Only keep the beacon light of God's love in our hearts, and wave the flag of individual thought and true worth in our lives, and by-and-by our own prosperity will teach others that we believe in a law of compensation, and that God's laws are so immutable, that right must triumph, and you will at least be satisfied with yourself. No belief can make one satisfied with him or herself, without a consciousness of right and wrong; and the human face bears the impress of the spirit within, and like the face of the clock, bears sure indication of the regularity of one's life. When we hear any one say, they do so and so, because they think it is right; the God within will always teach their spirit the correct way.

Coming into my office one day, very tired, and planning in my mind to lie down as soon as I could, my girl said, "there is a woman wants to see you," it rose to my lips to say, "I cannot see another patient to-day;" but duty, that stern master, kept me silent, and I passed into the office, and found a woman sitting there waiting for me. She wore a large wide ruffled cap upon her head, a shawl thrown hastily about the shoulders, and when I said, "what is wanted," she looked up and exclaimed, "are you the woman that cures folks?" I said, "I try too, sometimes." "Well," she said, "me old man is very bad, and no one can help him; they say he must die. But I heard of the likes of ye, and come at onct." "Have you had other physicians," I asked. "O, yes; we've had four," giving me the names of well known physicians. "Well," I replied, "you certainly have had enough to kill him; four physicians from Monday morning till Friday noon; but I will go and see what I can do." I followed her, and truly had no heart in the matter, I was so tired; and besides I had determined not to take foreigners in my practice; but the woman's grief-stricken face, enlisted my sympathy, and as we walked along, she told me that they said he must die. "But he's been a good old man to me, and I want to do all I can for him," said she.

Arriving at the house, I went up a flight of stairs into a square room, where were a dozen or more women talking. I passed through into a bed-room, and beheld a man about sixty years of age on the bed, going from one side to the other in agony. I placed my hand upon his forehead, and said to the woman, "what is this man's name?" "Be sure, ma'm, it is my husband, Mr. E." I said, "Mr. E., if you will be quiet a moment, I will tell you what the trouble is;" and I told him. It was congestion and inflammation of the kidneys. I called for a quart of water, cup of salt, jug of hot water put to his feet, and turned to put some medicine in a tumbler to give him to drink, when I beheld a Catholic priest in spirit, holding up to me a cross, and smiling to me. I placed a goblet to the sick man's lips, in which I had dissolved a powder, then bowed to the spirit priest my thanks, and as it was four o'clock P. M., turned to the wife and said, "I will see him again this evening," and left.

In the evening, when I called, I never ascended stairs with such forebodings, and it was only the desire to see the priest again, that gave me any encouragement for my patient; but when I passed through the first room, I felt that there had been a change, and when I passed into the bed-room, the first greeting was, "it's welcome ye be, for ye've taken the heat all out of me;" and the pipe, which he was smoking, went under the pillow at once. I gave medicine, and orders for the night, when he looked up to me and asked, "when shall I get relief from this terrible suffering?" At that time, the priest I had seen before, came up to me and said, "say two o'clock to-night." I turned to the sick man, and said, "two o'clock to-night." Then telling his wife I should remain in my office to-night, as I have many sick patients, and if your husband gets entire relief, come and ring my door bell, as I shall be anxious about him, and went home. And at five minutes past two that night, she rang my bell, and said he was easy and sleeping, as nature had assumed her natural conditions.

I went the next morning, and found my patient waiting anxiously for his breakfast. As I came out of the house, the priest approached me, and on the cross which he held out to me, lay a crown, and looking up into my face said, "no cross, no crown," and passed from sight.

I have never seen those persons since, but know the man is living; and in three days from that time, he was at his business. What brought that priest there, and what he had to do with me, is a problem I leave to those who call us deluded, to solve; and who are so self-conceited, that they do not think that God has given His angels charge concerning us. But let me assure you, that they that seek shall find.

God's loving hand will guide our way;
And if we ask His tender care,
He will not fail us, but will prove,
That He is strong; the mountains He can move.

CHAPTER XXIII.

MAN'S PROTECTION TO WOMAN.

It has been said that "man's inhumanity to man," is beyond comprehension. If so, who can comprehend man's injustice to woman, and the terrible consequences that follow it? I do not expect this to apply to women who sit lazily at home, and are supported by their lords and masters. Ah! no, those are not the women I write of, but are made up ladies for the occasion, more like dolls, and quite as useless; but the true and sincere woman, who takes an interest in life, and tries to understand her duties, and realizes the responsibilities which rest upon her. My observation in life, and my experience as a woman and physician, and what I have gained from others, by their sad experiences, I have come to the conclusion, that man's protection to woman is a libel upon the name of protector. For in life woman would not need to be protected, if it were not for men. For when we fly from the bad man to the good to protect us physically, it is because we feel that they have more physical strength; and often find that to escape physical suffering, women leave a bad man, and rush to the protection of a good one, and find, too late, that they are only kept true, by the true and virtuous women they come in contact with. A young girl was in my office not long ago, that had suffered every thing from the abuse of a dissipated father, and bore the stripes upon her person, where he had inflicted blows to make her give her money to him. A so-called good man came one day, and took pity on her, and assisted her out of that terrible condition; but, of course, swamped her morally, for his kindness, and she came to me for advice. There are more Jennie C.'s than one, and many just such protectors. It is said "God placed every thing in subjection to man," and woman comes under the law; and why are not men held more responsible for these terrible acts? I will answer why. Men make laws to suit themselves, and women have to abide by them; but there will be a time when we shall all be where God's laws are universal, and man will find that he will reap as he has sown.

I was once obliged to go to New York on a night train, in answer to a telegram to see a sick patient; and being alone, felt perfectly safe. It was a very heavy snow storm; I laid my head on my muff, and went to sleep; when I awoke, I found that two gentlemen had moved over into a seat front of me. I got rested, and was ready to chat, even with strangers; one of them said to me, "you seem to take your journey very easy." I said, "yes, I am used to travelling." They then chatted upon various subjects. But one of them seemed very uneasy. He had not found out all he wanted to know. They asked what hotel I would stop at. I answered, "I have not yet decided."

When we arrived at Hartford, one of them remarked, "are you not afraid to travel on a night train, in a public car, alone?" "O, no," I said, "there are no wild beasts on the way, and all I have to protect myself from, is men; and I am amply protected from them always." Immediately one of these gentlemen handed me his card, — the uneasy wretch who had thrown out so many insinuations. I looked at it and smiled; and when we arrived in New York, I took a carriage for the home of my patient, he still tagging at my heels. As I stepped into my carriage, I said, "you will give my respects to your wife, Mr. W., and say to her, that her husband tried to insult her doctor on the cars, and acted like any thing but a gentleman. But it is what we expect of such protectors." He was non-plussed, I assure you. I had seen his picture, and also his card before; his card had been sent to me many times to put on his wife's box of medicine.

I may say many bitter things on this subject, but I assure my reader I will not deviate from the truth. Much as I admire true manhood and true womanhood, just so much do I despise that class of men, who, like vampires, are destroying every weak woman that comes in their way, and use every means in their power to get an influence over them, and they escape, and leave their victim to weep.

What are our scientists about, with all their knowledge, that they have never sent out a warning voice to the masses, concerning this subtile *curse*, animal magnetism, that so many men are using every day to lead to ruin the weak women whom it is their duty to protect?

I knew a young woman, whose husband ill-treated her, because she would not receive the attention of an old "libertine," that he might be hired to work by the year. She never forgave him, and when her children had grown up, she left him, and all her neighbors pittied the poor man with such a wife, when he had drank and gambled so, that he was willing to sell his own wife. What do you think of the seller and buyer, both husbands and fathers, and woman's natural protectors? I am also acquainted with a lady, who sews every night till twelve o'clock; rises again in the morning, who left her husband because he spent all his earnings drinking and playing dominoes, loafing in bar-rooms, or on the wharves, Sundays, and the society to which she belonged, scandalized her so, that she was obliged to return to him to save her good name.

I have had girls tell me, that when they have been seeking honest employment, and apply to men of different firms, and would say, "why, we cannot work for so little," the man would look them in the face and say, "you must get some gentleman to pay your room rent." What kind of protection is that? Crush woman down on wages, and force them to travel the street, to keep from starving and freezing, and then make a law to have them arrested by your immaculate police. And if I was the only woman living who dared to speak, I would tell the truth on the subject; for it is infamous, that women are preyed upon in such a manner, by those who call themselves protectors. If you find a woman that follows man's examples, and turns vampire, is it to be wondered at that the lords of creation should be whipped once in a while with their own weapons?

My advice to my sisters is, put forth all the energies God has given you. Be self-reliant, cultivate moral courage, fear nothing, love God, and maintain your own individuality. It is the best protection woman can have, and you need not fear the result. You will make a better wife, better mother, and command the respect of mankind, and the love of women. That is all the world can give; for it is the weak-minded mothers that have been kept in subjection, that has filled our world with woe.

Bless God, that through the open door of inspiration, woman can learn her rights, and exercise her abilities, in spite of opposition; a new era has commenced, and if we have fought step by step, for our position, we have no one to thank for our advancement, but God.

CHAPTER XXIV.

ANIMAL MAGNETISM.

The vampireism of to-day is not confined to any one class, by no means; and I shall not write concerning what I do not know. But if there is one thing more than another, that scientists should make themselves acquainted with, it is Animal Magnetism; and every human being should be held rèsponsible for its use, or the abuse of it; for in the hands of the good and upright man or woman, it is a blessing. In the hands of evil-disposed, it is a curse. 1st. Because it is an outgrowth from mesmerism, which has power to control the will of an individual, while animal magnetism controls the will and the body also; leaving the spirit of the individual cognizant of the acts, without power to prevent them, or to exercise the will; and why God, permitted such a law, is more than my feeble mind can fully comprehend, unless, by the same law, that the beautiful sun that gives us light and life, by which we are all electrized, and everything is made to come forth, by its warming influence, and benevolent rays, will also destroy us, by burning up our very being, and scorch up everything that would sustain physical life, and also cause sickness and disease. The waters, which quench our thirst, keeps us alive, by the animal life in it; also cleanses our bodies from impurities; and our ships sail on its mighty waters, and yet it will drown us, and become our greatest enemy. The fire that warms us, and cooks our food, while we keep it under control, is our friend; but a terrible enemy, when beyond restraint. The moon, with her silver rays, and calm light, will poison our food, and destroy human life. So in thinking over all our blessings, I find they can all be turned to our disadvantage. Even religion, too much of it, unbalances the mind, and makes some persons believe, that to live a natural life, is a sin. I have known two persons, one of which was afraid to sin, even in thought, so made themselves wretched and all about them; and at last became an opium eater, and slept most of the time, fearing they might sin, in thought, if awake; while the other, was thoroughly demoralized, fearing nothing, and caring for no one; and there was not much choice between them; showing that we must keep a well-balanced mind to enjoy health or happiness, or make those happy around us. I was glad to learn that there was a law concerning mesmerism, and persons were responsible for the use they made of it. But animal magnetism is used so indiscriminately, that its results are not much known. Yet the world is full of its sufferers. There is hardly a day passes, that we do not hear of some very strange and peculiar occurrences taking place, of persons being led by others, into all kinds of unlikely actions which is the cause of much unhappiness; and they really cannot underseand it themselves; and yet there is a class who understand its workings, and practice it upon all they come in contact with, to their harm. We declare that class of persons are dangerous, and should be held responsible.

I have known vampires, in the shape of men, to use their magnetism upon innocent women. Many an innocent girl is led to her destruction, for it is not necessary for the person to be present, in exercising animal magnetism. After it is once thrown upon them, in the most trifling way, they can be led, and not realize it themselves. I know a lady who was affected by a friend of her husband's, who would will her to meet him, when the pure wife would be frantic; and she sent for me to come and see her. She had locked the door of her room, and thrown the key out of the window, to prevent going out, she so utterly despised the man; and his being the friend of her husband, he would not believe anything against him. The country is filled with such "vampires," and some persons get their power by using manipulations on their patients.

Some willl give their money, and other valuables, to those who exercise the power over them. I had a patient once so ill, that she could not sit up all day. I would leave her in bed, and go out to attend to my patients, when on my return she would be missing. She would go to meet a gentleman, be gone till the next day, and when she returned, would sit and cry for two days. He married her, but no doubt will see his wickedness visited upon him before he dies; but as he was just to her at last, I have wondered if he knew that he ruined her health by so doing. Many strange and singular incidents occur, which produce insanity from this cause, and it sometimes goes under the name of Love. Pshaw! there is no love about it; and if the victim once mistrusts the person is trying to exert an influence over them, the most fearful hatred takes its place. Nature never intended coercive measures in love affairs. Love is the blending of two souls, while this power is the positive over the negative.

I know a lady who was in the habit of going to a store for her many purchases, and in talking to a clerk, one day, had her bundle sent to her house. Not long after, one Sunday evening, she felt that she must go out. Upon going out, she noticed this clerk nearly opposite the house. He nodded, and she passed on to see a friend; on returning, in about an hour, she met him again, but thought nothing of it. In a few days she went to a strange meeting, and to her astonishment, he was there. The next week she went to the store, as was her wont to do, and after doing her shopping, stepped into a cafe, for lunch, and to wait for me; but who should walk in but this same clerk, and she began to be terrified, feeling that he was trying to exert an influence over her, and spoke of it to me; and for a long time never went out without company of her husband, and so broke the chain that that "vampire" was weaving around her.

Husbands, be loving and kind to your wives. No third person can come between you and your wife, if there is true harmony, and you do not take some friend to turn vampire on you and yours. I once had a pet cat, and also a pet dove; and one day I heard my dove moaning, and noticed it flying round a tree, and every time it went round, the dove would come lower and lower. I wondered what was the matter, when in the grass I beheld my cat, magnetizing the dove, and in so doing, gained a will-power over the dove, until she would have brought it within her reach. I caught up a stick and struck the cat, and killed my poor little dove. "The reason why" is, that the cat had so thoroughly magnetized the dove, that in striking the cat, the shock killed the dove.

Let this teach human beings, that magnetism is not any thing that can be trifled with, neither by men or women. Let no one get an undue influence over you;

and if you find they have, exercise your own will, and throw it back upon them ; and aspire to God, and his ministering angels will assist you. I knew a lady who came near losing her life by one of these "vampires." She was quite ill, but in health was a very positive woman, and very much interested in all the sciences. A strange gentleman called on her, on business. While there, he said "he was a phrenologist." A lady present suggested that the sick lady have her head examined. The lady not refusing, as she had many very wonderful gifts, and was curious to see if he could tell any thing about them. But it seemed that the villain, for he proved to be such, had heard that the lady was a clairvoyant, and there had been a terrible murder committed, and he was anxious to get the one thousand dollars that was offered as a reward for the murderer; so, while examining her head, he placed his will-power on her, to send her after the dead body. And the lady, feeling some unusual effects from him, attributed it to the weakness, and the effect of the sick head-ache, from which she had been suffering; and it seemed he went away, and left the effects upon her; and coming in again, and seeing she was alone, and knowing that she was affected by his magnetism, tried to get her into his power. He had got control of her will and body, but could not control her spirit; and so did not get the desired information. For two weeks she could see a long, dark passage way, with a woman holding a light, and two men carrying a human body, though the villain would not throw it off from her, as he knew she could tell him if not opposed by her spirit-friends. What did he care? He did not believe in a future state, so he held her. But God never forsakes those who trust Him; and she sought three other persons to break his power over her. At last a physician, a good and noble man, came between her and his evil magnetism, and broke it, and by so doing, found a gifted woman as his wife, whose wonderful powers have been a blessing to them both, while she is blest with a kind and loving husband, to strengthen her in good works. So does God teach that evil will always be overcome with good; as good is positive, and evil negative. Evil may triumph for a time, but goodness and truth shall last for ever.

So, never give up, though your feet they may totter
Circumstances may sometimes lead you astray;
But bring up a will-power, and fight in the battle,
For God is all strength, He will not turn away.

And then when you win, your glory'll be brighter,
From the knowledge you've gained in the struggle with sin,
But don't mind the scar, it may look bad and trouble,
But, remember, it's only a mark on the skin.

CHAPTER XXV.

DR. WINCHESTER.

Mediums cannot always tell who influences them, as there are days that many different influences may come to them, touch them, and not give them any idea who they are. You might be sitting in a very dark room, and any number of persons come silently to you, and place their hand upon your head, touch your hand, smooth your hair, and even whisper loving words to you, imprint a kiss upon your cheek, and you not seeing them, could not take your oath who they were; but, at the same time, no one could convince you that you had not felt their touch, as when you cannot see, the sense of feeling is very acute. So it is with mediums. Then there are others. When they lay their hands upon you, they say, "I am Willie, or Nellie," or whatever their name may be; so you will know at once, and it is so pleasant to get the name, but it is not essential to prove the law of communication.

My first control was Dr. Kittridge, as a medical instructor. He examined diseases through me for eight years. Then he informed me that he had taught me as far as he was able, and brought to me a new teacher, Dr. Winchester. I felt very bad about it, feeling that I had lost a dear friend; but soon learned to like the influence of Dr. Winchester, and he has been my medical guide for twelve years, for which I render him many thanks. To be convinced of the change, I wrote to Mrs. Webb, of New York city, a lady I did not know, who has her communications come on a closed slate, she only placing her hands on the table; I asked her to sit, and call my guides. I then told them, (the guides,) to go there, and answer my questions, and give the name of my new guide. When the answer came, it was signed by Dr. Winchester. At one time I was awakened at four o'clock in the morning, and asked to get up and prepare some medicine for a Mr. L., at City Hall. I was surprised, but Dr. Winchester said, "we cannot lose L. quite yet, I will send for it at seven to-night." I did as directed, but smiled when I thought of it. At seven L. came and said, "What have you for me?" I asked "what he meant." "Well, I am to have some medicine from Dr. Winchester, to help me." He then told me that he was sick the night before, and was told to come and get his medicine.

I must answer a question here that is often asked of me: "Why do spirits take uneducated persons to do their work through?" Because those persons having an education, so much of it is false, and the mind so prejudiced, that it is almost impossible to impress them strong enough to drive out that which they have become opinionated in, and so they rather educate a person in their own way, especially in the administering of medicines, or in theology; as one is to be given to the body, the other feeds the mind, and both are essential to a well directed life; as the morals depend very much upon the condition of mind and body. When they have educated the person, in all that is necessary to the promotion of health, and learned them the simplicity of adapting remedies to the human body, and know that they are a success, they consider them well qualified in their work. Then the professors leave them with a psycological control, and turn their attention to other students. This is why there is so much difference in the success of clairvoyant physicians. The reason is because their organizations are not developed to be physicians. Mediums should understand this; to be successful as a physician, requires a well-balanced brain, and to be a natural chemist. The trouble with your physicians to-day is, they are too dependent upon secondary knowledge, and use medicines compounded by chemists who do not understand anything concerning disease. No poison should be given to human beings. Do they not take enough in the food they are obliged to eat? Surely they do!

Theology will be obliged to step down and out. So will physicians be obliged to take their own poisons, and if need be, die from the effect; as there are millions of spirits coming to earth, to clear the poisonous filth that is thrust upon the human race, not only destroying the body, but retarding the growth of the spirit. So do not be alarmed! Spirits of the celestial world are descending to your earth, like snow-flakes, all individualized; but as soon as they reach your atmosphere, they unite in one great work, and will in time clear the malaria of poison out of your midst; and then theology will weep, and wail, and gnash its teeth, and the chain of satan will be broken, which has bound you three thousand years.

It is the cause of some anxiety in the ecclesiastical world, that their churches are diminishing in numbers. Be that as it may, they have not wandered far, as all spiritualists come out of the churches; and if they were perverted in their spiritual views, spiritualism is not to blame; but your "lost sheep" will be found, my friends, in the Fold of Spiritualism, at least twelve millions of them!

God's laws are slow, but never mind,
His power is all the same;
But what he grinds is exceedingly fine,
And we are not to blame.
If we are chosen to do his work,
We must not look behind;
The wheels will move, and we be crushed,
And ground exceedingly fine.

CHAPTER XXVI.

SPIRITUALISM.

Spiritualism is the true demonstration of spirit out of the body, while Christianity is a faith in spiritual things, without positive knowledge. The honest investigator will most surely find truth, and knowledge, in spirit communion, if they are only patient, persevering, truthful, and honest themselves. No one is expected to find the "pearl of great price" everywhere they seek it, but that is no reason that it is not to be found. If persons are patient for years accumulating great fortunes, how much more patient they should be in gaining such knowledge as will lift them out of the theological perdition for an eternity. The manifestations of spirits is a truth, that no sensible man or woman should dare gainsay, in a time like the present, and would only expose their ignorance of the law of inspiration in trying to refute it, and show to an intelligent people that they were behind the times, in at least, the most essential knowledge concerning a science which is moving the whole world. Men may make great fortunes by over-reaching one another, but to understand a science that learns us to live here, and to take the best possible care of your bodies, is the fortune we should most eagerly seek. "Money taketh to itself wings and flieth away," but the science of Spiritualism teaches us how to live here on the earth, and that knowledge can be taken with us to spirit life. Let others say, and believe what they may, *I know*, beyond a doubt, that spirits do communicate with mortals; that they can rap, touch, control, influence, impress, psycologise, appear, materialize, and write and talk to us, all under proper conditions, after they have left the human body; but that they cannot do so at haphazard, I am well aware. Suppose a case: I wished a beautiful mansion built, and went to a contractor, and he agreed for a certain sum to build said mansion, but I was not willing for him to use his own conditions. He must not have an architect, nor a mason, carpenter, plumber, gas-fitter, painter, or any of the conditions required in house-building, but simply give him specifications; people would say I was an idiot, or crazy. Yet God gives our mediums power and special gifts, and persons expect to be benefitted by them, or understand them, without complying with any of the conditions necessary, and then cry fraud, or that we are deluded. There are no more frauds in the spiritualists ranks than there are ignoramuses out of it (in proportion to their numbers,) that think they know all there is to be known, when it would take more books than ever was printed on your earth to contain all we don't know. That spirits can influence persons for good or evil is proved in the bible, as well as by the manifestations of to-day, and if you aspire to be, and do good, your aspirations will be answered by inspiration, to elevate you and those you come in contact with, by producing harmony and sympathy · but if we allow our minds to become perverted, we will attract those inharmonious spirits, who enjoyed making trouble here in life, and prefer the low and evil propensities of their natures to still keep their spirits in bondage, and near the earth, and may dwell near the earth for years, feeding their natures by influencing human beings to perform their dirty work for them. Teach this truth to drunkards, and you will find it the best temperance lecture to all inebriates, as they will all tell you the same story. They cannot account for periodical drunkenness. But I say it is because they open the door by the habit of drinking, that lets the spirit have an influence over them, and they will run them until they use up all their vitality. Intemperate persons would do well to be warned by this.

The science of Spiritualism cannot be learned in a few months, but it takes years of thoughtful study, and no one but an honest person who can take knowledge gained by other investigators, but will be tired in their research, unless they are fortunate enough to be a medium themselves. No human being has a right to say what God has permitted to exist since the world began, is false, or uncalled for. Ignorance, bigotry, Christianity, have caused bloodshed enough, and crime, and murder runs riot in your world to not now have a religion that will teach men that there is no praying your sins out of sight, or of being absolved from them. The sins and the persecutions which have been perpetuated by the church are being now answered for, and Spiritualism, the white winged angel of peace, will yet spread her wings and soar from all your tabernacles of worship, and from your pulpits will the cry go forth, one God and Father, and universal love to all His children, with the gate of heaven left open that the tired and weary ones of earth may know that after this sojourn here, and duties done, there will be rest and peace, and no obstacles put in our pathway to prevent our progress. There are those who sneer at spirit rappings, and say, "*Our* spirit friends would be in better business than rapping on tables and walls." Now I see nothing disgraceful in raps, or tips. Do we not get our telegrams under the same law? It is no discredit to our spirit friends, but it shows how terribly ignorant our earthly friends are concerning the law of communication, either in this world or the other.

That tiny rap on my table has many times been

more to me than every friend I had in life, because I knew they were true; and I have talked with those unseen friends, and been answered by raps, in the still hours of night, when it has cheered my sad heart and given me strength for the next day's duties which no human being could have given me. For if earthly friends assist one another they never let them forget the obligation they are under to them; that is what destroys love and thankfulness, as the obligation becomes burdensome, and the apparent blessing is changed to a curse. Not so with our spirit friends, their love and sympathy strengthens with our sorrow, as it makes us need them more. I so thank God for the tiny rap that has told me many times I was *not alone.*

Men of means, feel it not only a duty but a privilege to help the weak ones of earth. Deal justly by those you employ, pay them what they are worth to you, and never lose sight of the fact, that all *in the earth or on the earth* belongs to God, and must be shared by all His children sooner or later, and when the wheel of events turns round, you nor your money, cannot prevent the equalization in the turning; for if you are just and honest yourself, you will throw that good magnetism upon those about you, and you will not be apt to find defaulters with you. But if in your inner life there is scheming and over-reaching, it will be felt by those in your employ and you wlll surely influence them to do the very thing which you fear, so is the law of God lashing you with a cane of your own making.

I cannot do the subject of Spiritualism justice, it is so grand and immeasurable, but I try in my own simple way to make it plain to my reader; for after I have joined the heavenly throng, I want to feel that I have tried to lift the mantle of doubt and darkness from some of earth's children, and encourage them to come to the front and bring whatever experience they have, that through the interchange of thought we may become wiser and happier. I am convinced that men and women cannot be happy until they fully realize that their bodies are temples for the spirit, through which that spirit acts, and that it is their duty to keep the body carefully, and try to understand its needs, that the spirit may act in accordance with the law of harmony. How contented is the spirit within, when it has gained the knowledge that when strife and discord shall cease, each one will gravitate to a home of *rest* and *peace;* and when all doubt is removed concerning the next life, selfishness will not exist, for the soul will overflow with thankfulness, and our religion will come from within, instead of from without, and we shall then realize that all spiritual knowledge comes from God, and that we are as near Him to-day as in years gone by, and we need not return to the dark past, for the blessed present is ours. It has been the religion of the past to crucify the body, and in so doing people have transgressed every law of life.

Spiritualism teaches that the body needs recuperation and care, so that the spirit may learn wisdom, and not be clogged by a body without any of the proper faculties well developed. It does not disturb me in the least to know that there are those who ignore spirit communication, as I know positively that I have the daily assurance, and sooner or later, they too will be obliged to succumb to evidence that shall be beyond question; and I am now enjoying the first fruits of the great feast prepared for the people, and I thank God that He has let His mantle of love fall upon me. For twenty years, in my practice, I have been assisted by spirit influence; they have not done my work, to be sure; but they have given me information, quickened my mental, and stimulated my energies; and all I am, I attribute to my trying to be worthy of their counsel and love, and their watchful care over me. I shall never forget God and His mercies, but shall ever remember those untiring messengers of His love, by whom I have been sustained. And my success and lucrative practice of to-day, has come from hard study, and by the approval and dictation of my spirit friends. Although sorrow has been mixed in the cup which I have drank even to the dregs, yet I look back through the darkness of the past, and behold God's loving kindness and tender mercies have been around and about me, and I have a blessed faith to lead me on, a religion based upon a science everlasting as the rocks, my children in the spirit world beckoning me upward; my children on the earth hold me here while they need me, my mother, ever thankful that the angels thought her child worthy of their choice; brothers and sisters enjoying different opinions, but in God's own time will know that the gates are left ajar for all His children; a loving husband, who feels proud that he has been permitted to give strength and encouragement to a woman, whose moral courage has never deserted her; though the storms and tempests of life have roared around her, opposition has never been able to overcome; when the light was open to her view, and the many patients who have sought my advice, for their bodily ailments and their spiritual strength; all of these I will leave in God's loving care, knowing that as he has fed me from angels hands, inspired me by angels voices, and poured over me the inspiration of the Holy Spirit, so he will give them as they shall stand in need.

LOVE'S DISAPPOINTMENT.

It was cold, and drear and stormy,
  And, battling with ice and with snow,
I wandered so dazed and discouraged,
  Not knowing which way I must go;
But a thought in my soul, to the surface
  Came bubbling up out of the night,
With tremulous feelings, but certain,—
  Go appeal to those in the light.
Then I wended my steps on to Cambridge,
  To another soul, strong linked to mine,
By a law, that one mother had given
  To the world, *two lives at one time.*
I there met a sad disappointment;
  He had gone to his home far away;
I returned to my home, sad and weary,
  So heart-sick I hardly could pray.
But I left a kind word; tho' so heavy,
  My heart was near breaking, that's true,
I was tired of battling with trials,
  And I sought to seek comfort from you;
But, lo! no interest was taken,
  And a shudder comes into my soul,
When I think of relations so sacred
  Have all been bartered for gold.
Was it indifference led to the disclosure,
  That no interest in me or in mine;
Had prosperity filled all the niches?
  Was the soul sleeping then for a time?
Oh, no! but God in His goodness
  Heard a prayer that was sincere and true;
I never might have any riches,
  If it makes me as forgetful as you.

For sometimes when our friends have stumbled,
  And our hearts are trembling with fear,
We look to those who are able,
  And think they will give us some cheer.
But, lo! while they are willing to help us,
  They wish to punish the same,
And to reach the one that is guilty,
  They stab the one not to blame.
But Jesus, that God-given brother,
  Who nourished and watered the seed,
Came to tell us, Oh! love one another,
  Though our hearts and feet they may bleed.
So I crushed down the terrible feelings,—
  Like a serpent they coiled, round and round;
But at last I conquered; with gladness,
  They were dead, no motion or sound.
And I thank the giver of all goodness,
  For the strength to do what He willed;
That my spirit might not bear the blemish,
  And I say to my soul, "Peace, be still."
But now with the love from another,
  No dearer, but loving and kind,
Who came to my soul left a starving,
  And kept me from losing my mind.
May you never feel sad or lonely,
  Broken-hearted and left to repine,
Because your gold does not glitter;
  Mine, is the kind that never will shine.

MARCH 24, 1879.

LOVE'S REALITY.

Alone, amidst the storm and tempest,
And the sky, so dark and drear,
Came a voice, like some one calling,
Calling, "help! oh, do come here."

Then I listened and feared to follow,
Lest my feet might go astray,
For the darkness was so dense,
And I did not know the way.

To my soul there came a feeling,
Can I risk another's mind,—
To assist me in my trouble,
Is there any soul that's kind?

Then I, too, sent forth a message,
Calling loudly, "Help! this way."
A manly voice came forth in answer,
I am with you, come what may.

His noble presence gave me courage,
And my sad heart he soon did cheer;
What's the use of my abundance,
If your call I do not hear?

How I bless the day of darkness,
That was so sad and drear to me,
When I know by my experience,
Another's soul was good and free.

Roll ye on, dark, sad, and cloudy
Days, that never can come again;
I have known, by my experience,
You can only bring us rain.

For the love that was so hidden,
'Neath the busy stir of life,
Flashed upon me, like the lightning,
To subdue discord and strife.

Bless the hand that led me gently,
Bless the heart that ope'd to mine;
Bless the word he spoke so kindly,
Oh! God bless him, he is thine.

www.ingramcontent.com/pod-product-compliance
Lightning Source LLC
Chambersburg PA
CBHW020535270326
41927CB00006B/588

* 9 7 8 3 3 3 7 3 7 3 4 4 3 *